Canny Cooking

Other cookery books available in Pan

Batia Asher and Carole Robson **Canny Cooking**

Mrs Beeton **All About Cookery**

Kathleen Broughton **Pressure Cooking Day by Day**

Lousene Rousseau Brunner **New Casserole Treasury**

Savitri Chowdhary **Indian Cooking**

Gail Duff **Fresh all the Year**

Gail Duff's **Vegetarian Cookbook**

Gay Firth and Jane Donald **What's for Lunch Mum?**

Theodora Fitzgibbon **A Taste of Ireland** **A Taste of London** **A Taste of Scotland** **A Taste of Wales** **A Taste of the West Country** **A Taste of Paris** **A Taste of Yorkshire** **Crockery Pot Cooking**

Michel Guérard **Michel Guérard's Cuisine Minceur**

Antony and Araminta Hippisley Coxe **The Book of the Sausage**

Robin Howe **Soups**

Rosemary Hume and Muriel Downes **The Cordon Bleu Book of Jams, Preserves and Pickles**

Patricia Jacobs **The Best Bread Book**

Enrica and Vernon Jarratt **The Complete Book of Pasta**

George Lassalle **The Adventurous Fish Cook**

Kenneth Lo **Cheap Chow**

Claire Loewenfeld and Philippa Back **Herbs for Health and Cookery**

edited by R. J. Minney **The George Bernard Shaw Vegetarian Cook Book**

edited by Bee Nilson **The WI Diamond Jubilee Cookbook**

Marguerite Patten **Learning to Cook**

Jennie Reekie **Traditional French Cooking**

Evelyn Rose **The Complete International Jewish Cookbook**

Rita G. Springer **Caribbean Cookbook**

Constance Spry and Rosemary Hume **The Constance Spry Cookery Book**

Katie Stewart **The Times Cookery Book** **The Times Calendar Cookbook**

Marika Hanbury-Tenison **Deep-Freeze Sense** **Deep Freeze Cookery**

Batia Asher
and Carole Robson

Canny Cooking

A guide to over 200 quick and easy gourmet dishes

Pan Original
Pan Books London and Sydney

First published 1979 by Pan Books Ltd,
Cavaye Place, London SW10 9PG

ISBN 0 330 25874 5
Set, printed and bound in Great Britain by
Cox & Wyman Ltd, Reading

to our husbands and children with love

Contents

Introduction

A gourmet meal from a tin? It may sound a grand idea but, as we've discovered, it's quick, easy and fun to achieve. Of course, if you are one of those dedicated cooks, who, last thing at night, leaves various ingredients to soak in wine or water – having already prepared the stock the day before – and who picks the strawberries on the very day of a dinner party – well, this book may not be for you! But if you are a busy person, often confronted by unexpected guests, or if you have a large family to contend with, tins will often save the day and prevent you from flying into a frenzy of activity and panic: indeed, they will allow you to spend time with your family or friends rather than in the kitchen.

There is no denying that the produce of tins is regarded by some people as limited and tasteless, but in fact there is a remarkable and ever-growing variety of tinned food available. Because tinned food may not look particularly attractive it is important to enhance dishes by carefully slicing and chopping any additional ingredients you may use (vegetables, herbs, or whatever), and also to bear in mind colour combinations.

Familiarity with tinned products is of course essential if one is to use them imaginatively and make the most of the possibilities. Just as a conductor must know the sounds and characteristics of his orchestra to achieve the best results, so one must know one's tins to produce a good meal. A permanent and carefully selected stock is vital and we have given advice on how to build this up. There is also a section on herbs and spices, which are extremely important as often the secret of fine cooking lies in the subtle use of seasoning.

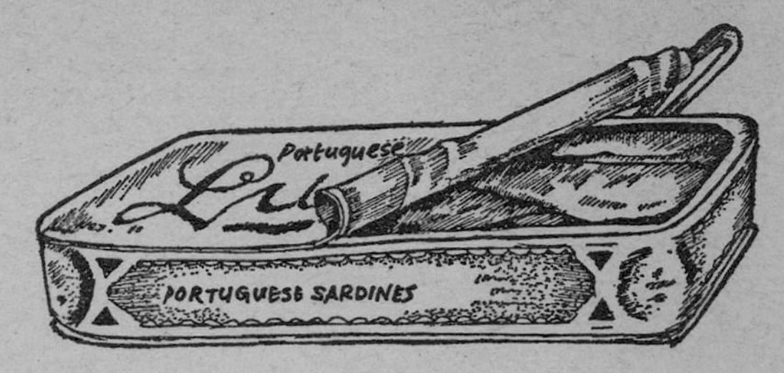

Economy, it must be stressed, is not our aim since in order to take the 'tinness out of tins' a number of more costly ingredients – such as cream, wine, nuts and fresh vegetables – are sometimes suggested.

Cooking is a living art and cooking with tins makes living easier. If one can remember that it is the final result, appealing to the eye and the nose and giving pleasure to the palate, that counts, you need never apologize about the source of your recipes. Indeed, your guests may never know.

The store cupboard – some useful hints

To get the maximum advantage out of tins a well-stocked store cupboard is essential. No reasonable menu can be prepared without certain key items and it is both time-consuming and irritating to have to rush out and buy them at the last minute. A well-stocked cupboard prevents panic expeditions, makes cooking fast, and life in the kitchen easier.

Tins do not need special storing in freezers, fridges or cool larders. Any kind of cupboard will do, even a chest of drawers – and there is nothing wrong either with stacking tins on open shelves or on the tops of cupboards as most tin labels are well designed and attractive enough to look at. Of course, if you do have a spacious, old-fashioned larder, so much the better.

The range and variety of the products you decide to stock will depend to a certain extent on your own personal likes and dislikes. But to organize your tins conveniently in groups is important. This way they will be easy to spot, easy to replace and the 'odd' tin won't remain unnoticed and unused for years. Incidentally most manufacturers advise that tins can be kept for up to two years.

To start your store cupboard off, we recommend a grand shopping spree. After that get into the habit of replacing missing items as you go along. Tinned products vary enormously in quality. Though the general standard is high, there is no doubt that certain manufacturers excel in certain foods. We found, for example, that there is very little to choose between fish products, whereas with meat there is considerable variation. For all products it is a question of taste, trial and error. When buying tins watch out for signs of rust, dents and bumps – all indications that the content may not be up to scratch.

The following is a comprehensive list for a well-stocked cupboard – in some cases it is sufficient to have one tin of a particular kind, in others it is as well to have several:

Your store cupboard for tins

Soups
asparagus
chicken broth
chicken and leek
consommé
mushroom
potato and leek
tomato
vegetable
Vichyssoise

Meat
beef chunks
chicken
corned beef
ham
meatballs
mince
pork
sausages
tongue

Fish
anchovy
cod's roe
herring
kipper fillets
mackerel
pilchards
prawns
salmon
sardines
shrimps
tuna

Vegetables
artichokes
asparagus
aubergines
beans:
  baked
  butter
  broad
  green
  haricot
  lima
  red kidney
  split peas
beetroot
carrots
celery
ladies' fingers
lentils
mushrooms
paprika
peas
pickled onions
pimentos
potatoes
ratatouille

red cabbage
rice
sauerkraut
spinach
stuffed vine leaves
sweetcorn
tomatoes
vine leaves

Purées and jams

apple
chestnut
honey
golden syrup
marmalade
raspberry
tomato purée

Fruit

apple slices
bilberries
blackberries
blackcurrants
cherries
chestnuts
cranberries
figs
gooseberries
grapefruit
grapes
loganberries
lychees
mandarins
mangoes
peaches
pears
plums:
- red
- Victoria

pineapple:
- crushed
- juice
- pieces

prunes
raspberries
strawberries

Miscellaneous

curry sauce
hoummous
macaroni cheese
Nestle's cream
spaghetti sauce
tahina
tomato and onion sauce
white wine sauce

In our recipes we have given the precise weights of the tins used. You may find small differences between brands. Within a 10 per cent variation, however, this shouldn't affect the recipe. Actually there is increasing standardization in tinned foods and these are the sizes you will find most widely used:

very small	115–200 g (4–7 oz)
Small	225–315 g (8–11 oz)
Standard	340–425 g (12–15 oz)
Large	450–500 g (1 lb and over)
Very large	680–750 g (1 lb 8 oz and over)

The recipes in this book are focused on tins but since dried foods and packets are also used and can easily be stored in the same places as tins, the store cupboard would not be complete without them. Again the following is a fairly comprehensive list:

Your store cupboard for dried foods and packets

Dried fruit
apricots
coconut
dates
prunes
raisins
sultanas

Nuts
almonds
cashews
peanuts
walnuts

Flour
corn
plain
self-raising

Pastas
cannelloni
pasta shells
rice
spaghetti
tagliatelli
vermicelli

Powders
cocoa
coconut
custard
drinking chocolate
gelatine

Sugar
castor
demerara
granulated
icing
soft brown

Savoury mixes
cheese sauce
chilli savoury rice
'coat-and-cook'
mashed potato
meringue
pancake
parsley
parsley and thyme stuffing
raspberry flavour dessert
rissole meat
shortcrust pastry
sponge cake
white mushroom sauce

Sweet mixes and packets
cooked apricots
digestive biscuits
flan case
ginger biscuits
jelly
jelly glaze
lemon pie filling
puff pastry
short pastry
sponge fingers
trifle sponges

Finally don't forget that such fresh ingredients as celery, mushrooms, onions, garlic and chives are always well worth having – as, of course, is fresh parsley, which will keep well in a plastic bag in the fridge or in water in a small jar. So when you're out shopping don't forget to keep a watchful eye on the vegetable counter.

Herbs and spices

Since herbs and spices are cheap and widely available we have incorporated them in our recipes wherever possible. Fresh herbs are generally preferable, but as herbs are both regional and seasonal you will often have no other choice than to use them dried. Always try to buy herbs and spices in airtight containers – at least as your first purchase, so that the containers may be kept for further use. Contact with air reduces a herb's aroma, so always replace lids tightly on spice jars and store in a dark place.

Black or white pepper and nutmegs should be bought whole and ground only as and when required – the aroma and flavour of pre-ground peppers bear no comparison to that of freshly ground. Although one can enrich a very ordinary dish with herbs and spices, remember that nothing spoils a dish so easily as over-flavouring; so always start by under-seasoning rather than over-seasoning – you can always add if you think it necessary. In fact an experienced cook rarely measures the flavourings and seasonings added. They are a matter of personal taste and practice. In recipes where we have suggested a specific quantity of seasoning, do taste to find out if it suits your palate, and vary accordingly. There are no rules as to which flavourings or seasonings should be added to a particular dish. The important thing is to see that they complement the basic ingredients and to be aware of the final harmony of the prepared dish.

Below is a list of the herbs, spices, and seasonings we have used. Small quantities of these should be kept in the kitchen and conveniently close to the cooker.

Herbs and spices

bay leaves
caraway seed
cayenne pepper
celery salt
chicken stock cubes
chilli powder
cinnamon
cloves
coriander seed
cumin seed
curry powder
dried mustard
French mustard
garlic
ginger
mace
marjoram
meat stock cubes
mint
mixed herbs
nutmeg
oregano
paprika
parsley
pepper (black and white)
salt
thyme
turmeric

Other seasonings

aspic jelly
Bovril
capers
chilli sauce
chutney
cocktail onions
cranberry sauce
horseradish
ketchup
lemon essence
lemon juice
malt vinegar
Marmite
mayonnaise
oil
olives
Parmesan cheese
rum essence
Soya sauce
tarragon vinegar
vanilla essence
wine vinegar
Worcestershire sauce

Imperial and metric equivalents (solids)

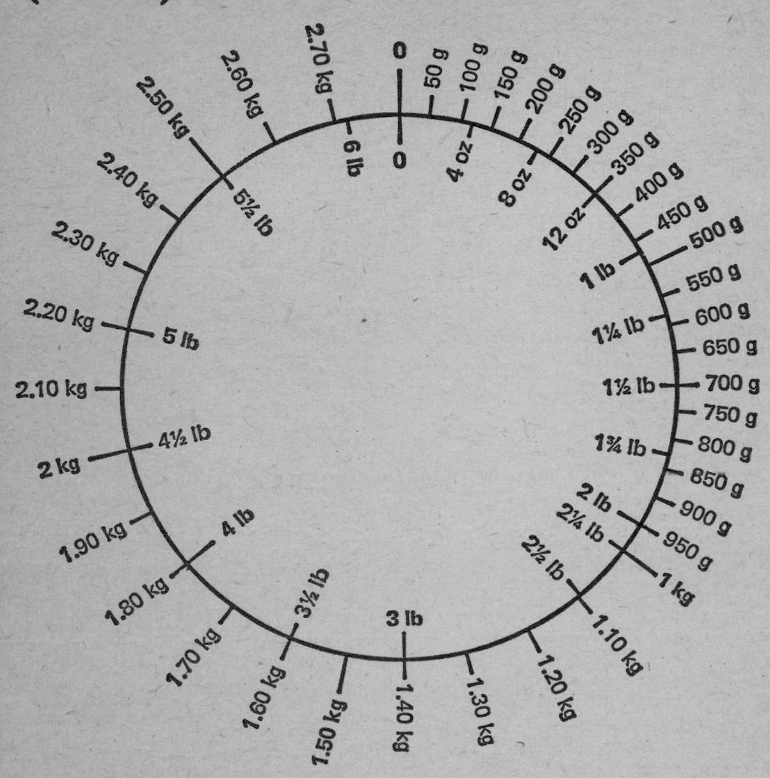

The weights and measures used throughout this book are based on British Imperial standards and the nearest workable metric units to keep the recipes in the right proportions.

International measures

measure	UK	Australia	New Zealand	Canada
1 pint	20 fl oz	20 fl oz	20 fl oz	20 fl oz
1 cup	10 fl oz	8 fl oz	8 fl oz	8 fl oz
1 tablespoon	⅝ fl oz	½ fl oz	½ fl oz	½ fl oz
1 dessertspoon	⅖ fl oz	no official measure		
1 teaspoon	⅕ fl oz	⅛ fl oz	⅙ fl oz	⅙ fl oz

Conversion of fluid ounces to metric

4 tablespoons (2½ fl oz)	= 70 ml (0.7 dl)
2 tablespoons (1¼ fl oz)	= 35 ml
1 tablespoon (⅝ fl oz)	= 18 ml
1 dessertspoon (⅖ fl oz)	= 12 ml
1 teaspoon (⅕ fl oz)	= 6 ml

(all the above metric equivalents are approximate)

Equivalents

1 UK (old BST standard) cup equals 1¼ cups in Commonwealth countries
4 UK tablespoons equal 5 Commonwealth tablespoons
5 UK tablespoons equal 6 New Zealand or 6 Canadian or 8 Australian teaspoons
1 UK dessertspoon equals ⅔ UK tablespoon or 2 UK teapoons
In British cookery books, a gill is usually 5 fl oz (¼ pint), but in a few localities in the UK it can mean 10 fl oz (½ pint)
Other non-standard measures include:

Breakfast cup	= approx 10 fl oz
Tea cup	= 5 fl oz
Coffee cup	= 3 fl oz

Oven temperatures

Food type	°C	°F	Gas No.	Oven heat
meringues keeping food hot	110°C	225°F	¼	very cool
fruit bottling	130°C	250°F	½	very cool
custards, egg dishes, milk puddings	140°C	275°F	1	cool
stews, rich fruit cakes	150°C	300°F	2	slow
slow roasting, plain fruit cakes	170°C	325°F	3	moderately slow
Victoria sponge cakes, biscuits, madeira cake	180°C	350°F	4	moderate
whisked sponges, small cakes	190°C	375°F	5	moderately hot
shortcrust pastry, tarts	200°C	400°F	6	hot
quick roasting, scones, bread	220°C	425°F	7	very hot
flaky and puff pastry, buns, rolls	230°C	450°F	8	very hot

Soups

If you ever have a nostalgic craving for that marvellous home-made soup mother used to make, remember that it involved long hours in the kitchen simmering meat bones and carcasses, then straining, chopping and adding. Our parents and grandparents may have been superb cooks, but they worked the hard way. Not only have times changed but time itself, or rather the lack of it, has become a dominant factor in our lives. That is why, when it comes to soups, tins are such a blessing – a welcome substitute for those hard and laborious hours.

There are many kinds of tinned soups available – perhaps more varieties than in any other product range. By using a tin of soup (or perhaps several different tins) as the foundation and carefully adding certain ingredients, you can create the taste and look of a home-made soup. Seasoning is of course important, as it does so much to improve the flavour; and because the appearance of a soup is important too, be sure to slice vegetables in attractive shapes. Remember when preparing a soup to relate it to the rest of the menu. If the main course is substantial, start with a consommé; if the main course is relatively light, a thick soup may be more appropriate. We've included all kinds of soups here – consommés and vegetable soups as well as regional specialities like Russian Borsch and Gazpacho. But whatever you choose make sure that you serve hot soups piping hot, preferably from a tureen at the table – slightly extra work perhaps, but it creates atmosphere and prepares your guests for good things to come.

Country-style vegetable soup

Serves 4–5

Time taken: 15 minutes

1 794 g (1 lb 12 oz) tin country vegetable soup with beef
For the stock: 1 chicken cube dissolved in 300 ml (½ pint) boiling water
1 medium-sized leek, thinly sliced
½ teaspoon parsley, chopped
freshly milled black pepper
2 tablespoons double cream

Tip the contents of the tin into a saucepan and pour in the stock. Add the leek and parsley and stir well. Season with pepper, bring to the boil and simmer for 5–10 minutes. Add the cream and cook for one more minute.

Carrot and butter bean soup

Serves 5

Time taken: 15 minutes

1 524 g (1 lb 2½ oz) tin whole carrots
1 425 g (15 oz) tin butter beans
1 medium onion, chopped
knob of butter
For the stock: 1 chicken cube dissolved in 300 ml (½ pint) boiling water
3 tablespoons milk
chopped parsley
salt and freshly milled black pepper

Drain off the liquid from the carrots and put into an electric blender together with the tin of butter beans. Blend for a few seconds. In a saucepan fry the onion in butter until soft. Pour the mixture from blender into the saucepan and add the stock, milk, parsley and salt and pepper to taste. Bring to the boil and simmer for a few seconds.

Soup with lima beans

Serves 6

Time taken: 10 minutes

The unusual combination of ingredients gives this thickish soup a distinctive flavour.

1 400 g (14 oz) tin vichyssoise
1 440 g (15½ oz) tin cream tomato soup
1 454 g (1 lb) tin fancy small green lima beans
1 medium onion, very finely chopped
For the stock: 1 chicken cube dissolved in 300 ml (½ pint) boiling water
freshly milled black pepper

Put all the contents of the tins into a saucepan, add the chopped onion and the stock, and season with black pepper. Mix well and bring to the boil slowly. Cook for a few minutes.

Curried split pea soup

Serves 3–4 Time taken: about 1 hour

It will not be necessary, as with most other dried vegetables, to soak the split peas in water overnight. You will, however, have to allow 40–45 minutes to cook the peas but you can do something else while these are on. The rest of the recipe is quick and easy – it should only take 10 minutes or so. Split peas are not available in tinned form.

225 g (½ lb) yellow split peas
generous knob of butter
For the stock: ¼ chicken cube dissolved in 350 ml (13 fl oz) boiling water
salt and freshly milled black pepper
1 level teaspoon Madras curry powder (or any fairly mild powder)
1 large hard-boiled egg, finely chopped

Put the washed split peas in a saucepan and cover them well with warm water. Cook with the lid on for about 40–45 minutes or until the peas are very soft. If during cooking the peas soak up all the water add a little more.

Mash the cooked peas as smoothly as you can using a fork or a masher but don't worry if some remain whole. they won't spoil the soup. Add the knob of butter, stir with a wooden spoon and gradually pour in the stock. If you find that the soup is too thin (it should be eaten quite thick) don't use all the stock. Season well with salt and pepper. In a bowl mix the curry powder with a little boiling water and stir into the soup. Taste to see if there's sufficient curry powder as brands vary a lot. Cook the soup on a low heat for 5–10 minutes. Garnish individual bowls with the chopped egg.

Pea soup

Serves 4

Time taken: 15 minutes

Try a tin of garden peas for this recipe rather than the ordinary variety, as they generally have more flavour.

2 knobs of butter
1 finely chopped onion
1½ tablespoons flour
For the stock: 1 chicken cube dissolved in 600 ml (1 pint) boiling water
1 283 g (10 oz) tin peas
salt and freshly milled pepper
finely chopped fresh or dried mint to taste
3 tablespoons double cream

Melt one knob of butter in a saucepan and fry the chopped onion for a few minutes until soft. Stir in the flour a little at a time and gradually pour in the stock whilst stirring all the time. When it has thickened, add the drained peas (reserving a few for later) and simmer for two minutes. Pour into a liquidizer and liquidize for a few seconds, return to the pan and cook for a minute or so. Season well, adding a knob of butter and the reserved peas as well as the mint. Bring gently to the boil and stir in the cream just before serving.

Mushroom soup

Serves 4

Time taken: 15 minutes

1 425 g (15 oz) tin mushroom soup
For the stock: 1 chicken cube dissolved in 150 ml (¼ pint) of boiling water
300 ml (½ pint) milk
225 g (½ lb) mushrooms washed and sliced
1 tablespoon of parsley, chopped
freshly milled black pepper

Empty the contents of the tin into a saucepan, stir in the stock and milk and gradually bring to the boil. Then add the mushrooms, parsley and plenty of black pepper. Stir and simmer for 5–7 minutes.

Cream of mushroom soup

Serves 4–5

Time taken: 15 minutes

1 small onion, finely chopped
generous knob of butter
1 213 g (7½ oz) tin grilling mushrooms in brine
2 tablespoons flour
1 chicken cube dissolved in 600 ml (1 pint) boiling water
150 ml (¼ pint) milk
salt and freshly milled black pepper
pinch of nutmeg
chopped parsley to garnish

Fry the onion in the butter until soft and then add the drained and finely chopped mushrooms. Fry for a few minutes then stir in the flour a little at a time. Blend in the stock followed by the milk. Season well with salt, pepper and nutmeg. When the soup has thickened reduce heat and simmer for 5–10 minutes. Garnish with a generous pinch of parsley.

Potato and leek soup

Serves 4

Time taken: 15 minutes

1 496 g (1 lb 1½ oz) tin new potatoes
300 ml (½ pint) milk
For the stock: 1 chicken cube dissolved in 300 ml (½ pint) of boiling water
1 large leek
large knob of butter
salt and freshly milled black pepper

Drain the potatoes. Purée them in an electric blender for a few seconds with half the milk and pour into a saucepan. Stir in the milk and chicken stock. Wash the leek thoroughly, cut into very fine slices and add to other ingredients. Bring gently to the boil, add the butter, pepper and salt to taste. Simmer for 5–7 minutes, stirring occasionally. Do not overcook the leek as it is particularly nice when firm.

Spinach soup

Serves 6

Time taken: 15 minutes

1 496 g (1 lb 1½ oz) tin leaf spinach
50 g (2 oz) butter
300 ml (½ pint) double cream
For the stock: ½ cube chicken stock dissolved in 600 ml (1 pint) boiling water
salt and freshly milled black pepper
juice of ½ lemon
1–2 hard-boiled eggs to garnish or a swirl of cream

Drain the spinach well, pressing down in a colander with a spoon to remove excess water. Put it in a saucepan together with the butter and simmer for a few minutes until well blended. Then purée the spinach in an electric blender and pour back into the rinsed out pan. Stir in the cream (leaving a little for garnish), pour in the chicken stock and season to taste. Add the lemon juice and simmer gently on a low heat until hot.

Garnish with either the reserved cream or finely chopped hard-boiled egg. To decorate, chop up an egg yolk and the white separately and arrange in a pattern over the soup.

Cold potato and spinach soup

Serves 4–6 Time taken: 7 minutes

If you have little time for cooking, this is the soup to make; it is creamy and delicious.

For the stock: 1 chicken cube dissolved in 300 ml (½ pint) hot water
1 538 g (1 lb 3 oz) tin jersey new potatoes, drained
1 496 g (1 lb 1½ oz) tin leaf spinach, drained
600 ml (1 pint) milk
freshly milled black pepper

Begin by dissolving the chicken cube in the hot water and leave to cool whilst you put together the rest of the ingredients. Into an electric blender put the potatoes and half the milk and liquidize for about 2 minutes until the potatoes have blended well with the milk into a very smooth, runny mixture. Then add the spinach but blend for only a few seconds so it is not reduced to a pulp – bits of spinach in fact give a nice texture to this soup.

Pour into a soup tureen, add the remaining milk, the cooled stock and season well with pepper. Stir thoroughly and chill before serving.

Red cabbage borsch

Serves 4–6 Time taken: 10 minutes

This is a popular Russian dish and the Russians like it very strong in flavour. The amounts indicated in this recipe, therefore, are for the stronger palate, so adjust the quantities of vinegar, salt and pepper if necessary.

540 g (1 lb 3 oz) tin red cabbage with apples
For the stock: 2 chicken cubes dissolved in 900 ml (1½ pints) boiling water
3–5 tablespoons wine vinegar
salt and freshly milled black pepper
1 142 ml (5 fl oz) carton soured cream

Open the tin and press the cabbage down with a wooden spoon and you will find all the excess liquid easy to drain off. Put the cabbage into a medium-sized saucepan. Pour in the chicken stock and mix especially well so that the cabbage is loosened and well soaked in the stock. Add the vinegar, salt and pepper a little at a time, tasting the soup as you go along and adjusting the seasoning.

Heat and bring to the boil then reduce heat and add the soured cream. Mix well and serve. If there are small lumps of soured cream in the soup it doesn't matter – in fact they add to the appearance and flavour. If you really want to indulge yourself, put in a second carton.

Beetroot borsch

Serves 6

Time taken: 15–20 minutes

1 284 g (10 oz) tin beetroot
2 heaped tablespoons pickled beetroot, drained
1 large onion, chopped
For the stock: 1 chicken cube dissolved in 300 ml (½ pint) boiling water
150 ml (¼ pint) milk
salt and freshly milled black pepper
soured cream to garnish

Empty the contents of the beetroot tin into a liquidizer together with the pickled beetroot and the onion. Blend for a few seconds. Pour into a saucepan and add the stock and milk. Season with salt and pepper, bring to the boil and cook for 5 minutes. Serve hot or cold in individual bowls adding a spoonful of soured cream to each serving.

Gazpacho

Serves 4–5

Time taken: 15 minutes

This lovely Spanish soup should be served ice cold. If it is required immediately, however, drop a few ice cubes in it as they do in Spain – it won't spoil the flavour.

1 396 g (14 oz) tin tomatoes
1 small onion, chopped
1 clove garlic, crushed
1 large green pepper, sliced
1 large slice of bread soaked in
1 tablespoon vinegar
salt and freshly milled black pepper
3 tablespoons oil
cucumber to garnish

Pour the contents of the tin into the blender together with the onion, garlic, green pepper, bread and the salt and pepper. While the blender is on, pour in the oil a few drops at a time, as for mayonnaise. When the ingredients are thoroughly blended, taste the soup and season with a little more vinegar if required. If the soup seems thick, a little cold water may be added (this will depend to a certain extent on the brand of tinned tomatoes used, since some contain more juice than others). Pour into a tureen and chill in a refrigerator.

Peel and dice some cucumber and either put it straight into the tureen or hand round separately. Croûtons, chopped onion and peppers can also be served as accompaniments.

Creamed tomato soup with garlic

Serves 4 — Time taken: 10 minutes

Tomato soup has become part of our staple diet. To ring the changes a little here is a creamy, tasty variation with the emphasis on the garlic and parsley.

1 794 g (1 lb 12 oz) tin creamed tomato soup
2–3 tablespoons parsley, finely chopped
2–3 garlic cloves, crushed
½ teaspoon dried powder celery seeds
large knob of butter
salt and freshly milled black pepper
For the stock: 1 chicken cube dissolved in 300 ml (½ pint) boiling water

Put all the ingredients into a medium-sized saucepan, mix well, bring to the boil, check the seasoning, adding more if desired, and simmer for 5 minutes.

Serve with fresh granary bread and butter.

Tomato soup

Serves 6 — Time taken: 15–20 minutes

1 large onion, finely chopped
1 knob butter
50 g (2 oz) flour
For the stock: 1 chicken cube dissolved in 600 ml (1 pint) boiling water
1 794 g (1 lb 12 oz) tin tomatoes
300 ml (½ pint) milk
1–2 tablespoons lemon juice
1 teaspoon brown sugar
salt and freshly milled black pepper

Fry the onion in the butter until soft and stir in the flour a little at a time. Pour in the stock very gradually and continue to stir. Strain the tomatoes, then break them up with a fork and add them to the other ingredients in the pan. Stir in the milk, followed by the lemon juice, sugar and salt and pepper, and bring to the boil. Cook for 2 minutes.

This soup is particularly nice served sprinkled with grated cheese.

Spicy tomato soup

Serves 6 — Time taken: 15 minutes

1 794 g (1 lb 12 oz) tin plum tomatoes
2–3 garlic cloves, chopped
1 large onion, chopped
2–3 tablespoons oil
For the stock: 1 chicken cube dissolved in 600 ml (1 pint) boiling water
1 140 g (5 oz) tin tomato purée
chopped parsley
pinch of dried oregano
salt and freshly milled black pepper

Separate the tomatoes from their juice. Keep the juice in a bowl and put the tomatoes into a liquidizer, together with the garlic, and blend for a few seconds. In a saucepan fry the onion in oil until soft, then add the stock gradually and stir. Add the tomato juice, tomatoes from the blender and tomato purée. Mix thoroughly. Sprinkle with parsley and oregano and season to taste. Bring to the boil and simmer for 2–3 minutes.

Asparagus soup

Serves 4–6

Time taken: 15 minutes

For the stock: 1 chicken cube dissolved in 600 ml (1 pint) boiling water
2 tins asparagus tips
1 packet asparagus soup
300 ml (½ pint) milk
freshly milled black pepper

Make the stock in a medium-sized saucepan. Add the contents of the two tins and the packet of soup. If the asparagus tips are too large cut them into smaller pieces before adding them to the stock. Mix well and make sure no lumps from the packet soup remain. Add the milk and season with plenty of pepper (more often than not tinned food is sufficiently salted already). Now bring to the boil and simmer for 2–3 minutes.

Chunky asparagus soup

Serves 6

Time taken: 15 minutes

1 340 g (12 oz) tin asparagus cuts and tips
For the stock: ¼ chicken cube dissolved in 300 ml (½ pint) boiling water
1 340 g (12 oz) tin asparagus spears
knob of butter
salt and freshly milled black pepper
soured cream to garnish

Purée the contents of asparagus cuts and tips in an electric blender, pour into a saucepan together with the stock and the liquid from the tin of asparagus spears. Bring gently to the boil and simmer for a few minutes.

During that time cut the asparagus spears in half longways and then into thin strips. Add them to the soup, together with the butter and salt and pepper. Add soured cream before serving.

Chicken soup with corn and green pepper

Serves 5–6 Time taken: 15 minutes

This soup is especially nice if the stock from a tin of whole chicken is used. See 'Chicken with Peaches and Wine', p. 70. Try and combine both recipes on the same menu or keep the stock in the fridge to use the next day. This soup can also successfully be made with stock from a cube.

generous knob of butter
1 small onion, finely chopped
2 bay leaves
For the stock: 1 chicken cube dissolved in 900 ml (1½ pints) boiling water
1 bouquet garni
salt and freshly milled black pepper
1 green pepper
1 340 g (12 oz) tin sweet corn
fresh parsley, finely chopped

Melt the butter in a saucepan and add the onion and bay leaves. When the onion begins to turn brown pour in the stock, add the bouquet garni and season with salt and pepper. Wash the pepper, then cut it up into small square pieces and drop them into the saucepan. Simmer for five minutes. In the meantime, open and drain the corn and add it to the pan. Cook on a low heat for another five minutes but no longer – the vegetables in this soup must not be overcooked; they should remain crisp and firm. Sprinkle some parsley over the soup before serving.

Chicken broth with leeks and potatoes

Serves 4–6 Time taken: 20 minutes

We derived a great deal of satisfaction from making this particular recipe as it is a good example of how a rather tasteless and insipid broth can be transformed into a good and wholesome home-made soup. Note that slicing the vegetables into attractive pieces – not overcooking them, so they remain crisp and retain their flavour – makes all the difference.

2 425 g (15 oz) tins chicken broth with leek
1–2 medium-sized leeks, washed and finely sliced
2 medium-sized potatoes, very thinly sliced
For the stock: 1 chicken cube dissolved in 600 ml (1 pint) boiling water
large knob of butter
freshly milled black pepper

Pour the contents of the two tins into a medium-sized saucepan and add the prepared leeks and potatoes. Pour in the stock and add the knob of butter. Season well, bring to the boil and simmer for about 10 minutes, stirring occasionally.

Chicken soup with mushrooms

Serves 4 Time taken: 10 minutes

This clear and light soup can be served on more formal occasions and is particularly nice if good-quality tins are used.

2 397 g (14 oz) tins clear chicken soup
6–10 small mushrooms, thinly sliced
a pinch of oregano
freshly milled black pepper

Tip the contents of the tins into a saucepan and bring to the boil. Then drop in the mushrooms, the pinch of oregano and season with pepper. Simmer for 10 minutes and then serve.

Chicken and leek soup

Serves 4–6 Time taken: 10 minutes

This is a thick and delicious country-style soup; it is ideal served in winter.

2 425 g (15 oz) tins chicken broth with leek
1 170 g (6 oz) Nestle's cream
4 leeks
freshly milled black pepper

Empty the contents of the two tins of soup as well as the cream into a medium-sized saucepan and stir with a wooden spoon. Then wash and trim the leeks thoroughly, cut them into thin slices, and add them to the soup. Season with plenty of pepper, bring to the boil and simmer for 5–7 minutes, stirring occasionally.

Chicken broth with garden vegetables

Serves 4 Time taken: 15 minutes

1 425 g (15 oz) tin chicken broth with garden vegetables
1 leek, finely sliced
300 ml (½ pint) milk
1 teaspoon Bovril
freshly milled black pepper

Empty the tin's contents into a saucepan, add the sliced leek and bring to the boil. Now reduce the heat, add the milk and Bovril, season well with pepper and stir. Simmer for 10 minutes before serving.

Consommé with egg and vermicelli

Serves 4 | Time taken: 15 minutes

1 397 g (14 oz) tin consommé
1 egg
50 g (2 oz) egg vermicelli

Empty the contents of the tin into a saucepan. Beat the egg lightly in a bowl and pour into consommé. Bring gently to the boil stirring all the time. Drop in the vermicelli and cook for 2 minutes.

Consommé with pork and peas

Serves 4–6 | Time taken: 10 minutes

½ 454 g (1 lb) tin sweet cured pork shoulder
1 425 g (15 oz) tin garden peas in water sugar and salt, drained
1 425 g (15 oz) tin beef consommé
300 ml (½ pint) hot water
freshly milled black pepper
4–5 heaped tablespoons toasted wheatflakes (from a packet)

Chop the pork into very small cubes and put them into a medium-sized saucepan. Add the peas, beef consommé and water and season with black pepper. Bring to the boil and after simmering for three minutes throw in the wheatflakes. (Don't put them in earlier or they will overcook.) Stir well and cook for another five minutes.

Serve with hot garlic bread.

Hors d'oeuvres

When you're surprised by unexpected visitors – and who isn't from time to time – you'll find this section particularly useful. In it we've included cold and hot starters, appetizing salads, pâtés and dips – all of which can be used either to accompany a drink or as a first course. Virtually all these recipes can be rustled up quickly, a great bonus which will allow you to join in on the drinks or to get on with preparing the rest of the meal in a relaxed way, knowing that appetites have been temporarily relieved. People with 'starving' children, who can never wait until a meal is ready, will also find this section very handy.

Eggs Florentine

Serves 4 Time taken: 30 minutes

This is a delicious and quickly prepared dish which could be served either as a starter or as a main course. Allow 2 eggs per person for the latter.

1 496 g (1 lb 1½ oz) tin spinach purée
50 g (2 oz) butter
½ teaspoon ground nutmeg
salt and freshly milled black pepper
4 eggs
For the sauce: knob of butter
1 tablespoon flour
300 ml (½ pint) milk
sprinkling of nutmeg
75 g (3 oz) grated cheese
2 tablespoons double cream
salt and freshly milled black pepper

Drain the spinach thoroughly and put it in a saucepan together with the butter, and the salt and pepper. Simmer on a low heat while you make the sauce.

Melt the butter in a saucepan and gradually incorporate the flour and milk. Stir continuously until the sauce has thickened to avoid lumps. Now add the nutmeg, most of the grated cheese (reserve 1 tablespoon for later), and the cream, and season well. Mix one tablespoon of the sauce into the prepared spinach.

Switch oven to 190°C, 375°F or Gas No. 5.

Butter an ovenproof dish. Spread the spinach evenly in it; then, using the back of a spoon, make 4 hollows and crack an egg into each one. Sprinkle with salt and pepper and pour the sauce over the top. Spread the reserved cheese over the sauce, sprinkle with dots of butter, a dash of nutmeg and a final grind of pepper. Bake for 15 minutes.

Stuffed spiny vine leaves with yogurt

Serves 3–4

Preparation time: 30 minutes
Cooking time: 30–40 minutes

This popular Greek dish may be served hot or cold, and is particularly nice with a yogurt accompaniment.

300 g (11 oz) vine leaves in brine
1 115 g (4 oz) packet chilli savoury rice
juice of 1 lemon
3 tablespoons water
1 tomato, skinned and finely chopped
1 dessertspoon parsley, finely chopped
Cooking liquid for the vine leaves:
4 tablespoons oil
4 tablespoons water
juice of 1 lemon
Yogurt preparation:
1 small carton plain yogurt
½ teaspoon bottled mint sauce (or fresh)
1 dessertspoon oil
salt and a little freshly milled black pepper

Open the tin of vine leaves and tip the contents into a colander. Separate the leaves one by one, then swirl cold water over them. Let them drain and partly dry off for a little while – they'll be easier to fill if not too wet.

Tip the contents of the packet of rice into a bowl, add the lemon juice, the three tablespoons of water, the tomato, the parsley and the salt. Mix the ingredients thoroughly.

Now spread about ½ teaspoon of the rice mixture into the reverse part of each vine leaf, fold in the sides first, then roll it up tight. Pack the stuffed leaves close together into a small saucepan and sprinkle them with a little salt. In a mixing bowl, blend the oil, water and lemon juice and pour over the vine leaves. Simmer on top of the stove with the lid on for 30–40 minutes. While cooking the leaves should be more or less covered with liquid but, should it reach a low level, add a little boiling water.

To prepare the yogurt, put it in a serving bowl and stir in the mint, oil, and salt and pepper. Hand round separately as an accompaniment for the hot or cold vine leaves.

Stuffed vine leaves in tomato sauce

Serves 6 — Time taken: 15–20 minutes

This recipe will turn already prepared stuffed vine leaves from a tin into a more interesting and tasty dish – a useful time-saver if other elaborate oriental dishes are to follow.

1 694 g (1 lb 12 oz) tin tomatoes
1 medium onion, chopped
3 garlic cloves, finely chopped
2 tablespoons oil
plenty of chopped parsley
salt and freshly milled black pepper
2 tablespoons red wine
1 369 g (13 oz) tin stuffed vine leaves

Empty the tomatoes into a liquidizer and blend for a few seconds. In a saucepan fry the onion and garlic in oil until soft and then add the liquidized tomatoes. Add the parsley, salt, pepper and wine. Bring to the boil and simmer for 2–3 minutes. Put the stuffed vine leaves into the sauce and stir gently. Simmer for a few minutes. Serve with garlic bread.

Stuffed green peppers

Serves 4 — Time taken: 45 minutes

Stuffed vegetables always look attractive so make the most of green peppers when they are plentiful. They can be served as a main dish or as an *hors d'oeuvre*. Tinned minced beef may be used for the stuffing instead of tongue. The dish may be enriched by the use of tomato sauce (see p. 85).

4 medium fresh green peppers
For the stuffing:
1 170 g (6 oz) tin tongue
1 small onion, finely chopped
1 heaped tablespoon parsley, finely chopped
4 tablespoons cooked rice
salt and freshly milled black pepper

Before dealing with the peppers prepare the stuffing: take the tongue out of the tin and chop it finely. Put it into a bowl together with all the jelly left at the bottom or round the sides of the tin because this adds moisture to the mixture. Add the rest of the ingredients with plenty of black pepper but check carefully the amount of salt you add because the tongue may be sufficiently salty already. Mix well and put to one side.

Now blanch the peppers by dropping them in boiling salted water for a few seconds, then drain them and wash under cold water. Dry well with an absorbent towel or kitchen paper. Cut off the tops in a neat circle, remove the seeds and stand them in a deep ovenproof dish.

Preheat oven to 180°C, 350°F or Gas No. 4.

Fill up the peppers with the stuffing. If there is any stuffing left put it around the peppers in the baking dish. Remember to replace the tops of the peppers when baking because they help keep the flavour in and enhance the look of the dish. Cover with foil and bake in the hot oven for a minimum of 20 minutes but more if you like them soft. Before finally taking them out of the oven check with a skewer to make sure they are to your taste.

Mushrooms with soured cream sauce

Serves 4 — Time taken: 10 minutes

150 ml (¼ pint) soured cream
2 tablespoons milk
1 teaspoon lemon juice
salt and freshly milled black pepper
2 212 g (7½ oz) tins grilling mushrooms
spring onions (3–4 shoots)
1 celery stick

Beat the soured cream in a bowl then add the milk, lemon juice and salt and pepper to taste. Drain the mushrooms thoroughly, slice them thinly and put in the bowl. Chop the onions and celery very finely and mix in gently with the rest of the ingredients.

Mushrooms à la grècque

Serves 3–4 Time taken: 20 minutes

This *hors d'oeuvre* has a rich and lovely sauce and should be served with fresh crunchy bread.

4 tablespoons oil
1 small onion, finely chopped
2 garlic cloves, finely chopped
2 212 g (7½ oz) tins button mushrooms in brine
3 tomatoes, peeled and finely chopped (soak in boiling water straight away for easy peeling)
150 ml (¼ pint) white wine
1 heaped tablespoon tomato purée
2 tablespoons chopped parsley

Heat the oil in a small saucepan and gently fry the chopped onion and garlic until they begin to turn brown. Add the drained mushrooms followed by the peeled and chopped tomatoes. Stir well with a wooden spoon and cook for five minutes. In a small bowl mix the wine and the tomato purée together and pour into the pan. Cook on a fairly high heat for ten minutes or so until the sauce has reduced and thickened. Stir in most of the parsley (reserving a little for garnish later) and cook for 2 minutes. Chill before serving and garnish with remaining parsley.

Bean and anchovy salad

Serves 3–4 Time taken: 15 minutes

1 440 g (15½ oz) tin butter beans
1 50 g (2 oz) tin anchovy fillets
For the dressing:
½ teaspoon finely grated onion
½ tablespoon white wine vinegar
2 tablespoons oil
3 tablespoons double cream
1 heaped dessertspoon parsley, chopped

Drain the butter beans thoroughly and arrange in a dish. Mix all the ingredients for the dressing leaving a little parsley aside for garnishing. Pour the mixture over the beans and then cut the anchovy fillets lengthways in half and arrange in a criss-cross pattern over the beans. (Use a sharp knife as anchovies tend to break easily.) Garnish with the remaining parsley.

Foul medames (round broad beans)

Serves 2

Time taken: 15 minutes

This is a delicious and substantial dish which may be eaten either as an *hors d'oeuvre* or a main dish. It is eaten in many countries all over the Middle East and is especially popular with poorer families because it is cheap and nutritious. Serve with spring onions and oriental bread (pitta).

2 small hard-boiled eggs
1 425 g (15 oz) tin of foul medames (round broad beans), in salted water
generous amount of salt and pepper
4 tablespoons oil
2 dessertspoons lemon juice

The first thing to do is to hard-boil the eggs. Into a smallish saucepan, empty the contents of the tin of foul medames and simmer covered for about 10 minutes or until the beans are soft but not mushy. Do not allow all the water to evaporate as there should be a certain amount of liquid to this dish. Add a little boiling water if necessary. Now tip into a serving bowl and season generously with salt and pepper. Add two tablespoons of oil and let it soak through the beans but do not mix.

In a separate bowl, mash one egg with a fork (but not to a paste), add salt and pepper and mix in the other two tablespoons of oil as well as the lemon juice. Thinly slice the other egg. Now put the egg mixture over the beans and garnish with the egg slices. Hand round spring onions and pitta separately.

Spinach soufflé

Serves 4–6

Preparation time: 20 minutes
Baking time: 25–30 minutes

This spinach soufflé, a particular favourite, is a basic recipe for other vegetable soufflés as well. Although it looks complicated, do not hesitate to have a go as it's very easy once you get the hang of it.

For this recipe you will need some greaseproof paper and string.

1 496 g (1 lb 1½ oz) tin leaf spinach (or spinach purée)
For the sauce:
50 g (2 oz) butter
1 tablespoon flour
150 ml (¼ pint) milk
salt and freshly milled black pepper
pinch of mace
2 egg yolks
3 egg whites
2 tablespoons sesame seed
OR
1 tablespoon grated cheese mixed with 1 tablespoon breadcrumbs

Preheat oven to 190°C, 375°F or Gas No. 5. Place a shelf in the centre of the oven. Prepare a 17 cm (7 in) in diameter soufflé dish by rubbing the inside with butter. Now cut out a piece of greaseproof paper twice the height of the dish (this should stick up over and above the dish and is done to allow the soufflé to rise when baked) and long enough to go round it. Then wrap the paper round the outside of the dish and secure it with string.

You will now need two saucepans to work with: a small one to make the sauce and a medium-sized one for the spinach mixture. Place the well-drained spinach in the medium-sized saucepan making sure that it's well puréed (use a fork if necessary) and put aside.

In the small saucepan prepare the sauce by starting with the roux. This is done by melting the butter first then gradually stirring in the flour. Remove from heat, and then add a little of the milk; carry on mixing in the milk until the sauce is thick and smooth. Return pan to heat and pour the rest of the milk in a little at a time, stirring all the while. Season with salt and pepper. Bring to the boil and cook for a minute, then pour the sauce into the spinach pan. Add the mace as well as additional seasoning and mix well.

Beat the egg yolks into the mixture one at a time and in a separate bowl whip the egg whites to a firm snow. Add a little egg white to the pan first, then blend the rest in. Turn the mixture into the prepared soufflé dish. Sprinkle either with sesame seed or cheese and bread-crumbs mixed together. Bake for 25–30 minutes, remove the grease-proof paper and serve immediately – hot soufflés cannot wait.

Beetroot salad

Serves 2–3 Time taken: 10 minutes

This salad can be served either on its own as an *hors d'oeuvre* or to accompany the main course.

1 227 g (8 oz) tin beetroot
1 medium onion, finely chopped
2 garlic cloves, crushed
½ teaspoon caraway seed, crushed
2–3 tablespoons oil
salt

Cut the beetroot into smallish even squares and mix in the finely chopped onion, the crushed garlic and caraway seed. Add the oil and salt and mix well.

Sweet and sour bean salad

Serves 4–5

Time taken: 15 minutes

1 430 g (15¼ oz) tin red kidney beans, drained
3–4 medium-sized pickled cucumbers, finely sliced
1 heaped tablespoon mango chutney
3 spring onions, finely chopped
2–3 heaped tablespoons sultanas
4–5 dried apricots, finely chopped
4 tablespoons mayonnaise
1–2 tablespoons hot chilli sauce
½ teaspoon celery salt
salt and freshly ground black pepper

Put the kidney beans, pickled cucumber, chutney, onions, sultanas and the apricots together in a bowl. Make the dressing by combining the mayonnaise and chilli sauce together. Blend them well. Season with celery salt, salt and pepper. Pour the dressing over the salad and toss.

Peach and horseradish salad

Serves 6

Time taken: 15 minutes

12 lettuce leaves
1 822 g (1 lb 13 oz) tin peach halves
150 ml (¼ pint) carton double cream
2 tablespoons of horseradish from jar of creamed radish
salt and cayenne pepper
1 bunch chives, finely chopped

Arrange all the lettuce on a big platter – 2 leaves one on top of the other for each person, or, if you prefer, put them in individual dishes. Then place half a peach on each portion of lettuce and if you have any over divide them equally between the portions.

In a mixing bowl beat the cream until thick but not stiff; fold in the horseradish. Season with salt and cayenne pepper. Add half the amount of chives and put a generous dollop of the mixture on top of the peaches. Sprinkle over the remaining chives.

Prawn and celery salad

Serves 4

Time taken: 15 minutes

3 sticks celery, finely sliced
3–4 spring onions, finely chopped
1–2 pickled cucumbers from jar or tin, finely sliced
1 198 g (7 oz) tin prawns in brine drained and rinsed
3 tablespoons olive oil
1 tablespoon soya sauce
142 ml (5 fl oz) carton soured cream (optional)
salt and freshly ground black pepper

Place the celery, spring onions and cucumber into a bowl. Drain the prawns well and add them to the vegetables. Add the oil and soya sauce and season at this stage with pepper only. Mix well and taste. If additional salt is required, add it.

The salad – already delicious – can be made into something very special by adding soured cream. Serve chilled with bread and butter.

Prawns and mushrooms in vinaigrette

Serves 4 Time taken: 15 minutes

This is a good all-the-year-round *hors d'oeuvre* and is delicious with fresh granary bread and butter.

1 213 g (7½ oz) tin mushrooms
1 198 g (7 oz) tin prawns in brine
3–4 tablespoons olive oil
1 tablespoon wine vinegar
½ teaspoon salt
½ teaspoon freshly milled black pepper
2 garlic cloves, crushed
2 tablespoons fresh parsley, finely chopped

Drain the mushrooms and the prawns – remember to read the instructions on the tin of prawns as they often need rinsing before use. Finely slice the mushrooms then put them in a small salad bowl together with the prawns.

Now make the salad dressing in a separate bowl. Mix the oil and the vinegar together and season with salt and pepper. Add the crushed garlic and the chopped parsley and stir vigorously until the mixture thickens and the ingredients are well blended. Pour over the prawns and mushrooms and mix thoroughly.

Prawn and cucumber cocktail

Serves 5–6 Time taken: 15 minutes

1 198 g (7 oz) tin prawns in brine
¼ of a large cucumber
2 lettuce leaves
For the sauce:
4 tablespoons mayonnaise
1 tablespoon tomato purée or ketchup
1 tablespoon Worcestershire sauce
2 tablespoons double cream
a little lemon juice

Drain the prawns in a colander, rinse well and leave to drain while you get the rest of the ingredients together. Peel the cucumber, cut it into fairly thick slices and then dice them. Wash and cut the lettuce leaves into very thin strips and set aside.

Make the sauce by putting all the ingredients in a bowl and mixing thoroughly.

Now combine the prawns, the cucumber and the lettuce and tip into small individual glasses. Top with a generous amount of sauce and cool in a refrigerator before serving.

Tomatoes stuffed with prawns

Serves 6

Time taken: 15 minutes

6 large tomatoes
198 g (7 oz) tin prawns in brine, drained and rinsed
142 ml (5 fl oz) carton soured cream
6 green olives, stoned and finely chopped
a small bunch of chives, finely chopped
freshly milled black pepper

With a very sharp knife slice off the tops of the tomatoes and put them to one side. Scoop out the inside of the tomatoes on to a wooden board and chop finely. Put into a strainer to drain away the excess liquid and tip into a medium-sized bowl. Now add the prawns to the bowl together with the soured cream, the olives and three-quarters of the chives. Season with pepper and mix well, making sure that all the ingredients are well blended.

Fill the tomatoes with the mixture and sprinkle on top of each a little of the remaining chives. Replace the tops of the tomatoes and the dish is ready to serve.

Jellied shrimps with garden peas

Serves 4–6

Preparation time: 5 minutes
Setting time: 30 minutes

1 198 g (7 oz) tin shrimps in brine, drained
⅔ of 539 g (1 lb 3 oz) tin garden peas, drained
1–2 pickled cucumbers, finely chopped
½ teaspoon ground celery seed
freshly milled black pepper
1 sachet aspic jelly
300 ml (½ pint) hot, not boiling water

In a medium-sized bowl combine the shrimps, peas and the cucumber. Add the celery seed. Season with plenty of pepper. Salt is not necessary as both the shrimps and pickled cucumber provide seasoning. Dissolve the sachet of aspic jelly in the hot water. Mix thoroughly and pour over the shrimps and cucumber. Give a final stir to all the ingredients.

Put in a refrigerator to set. Serve with cold potato salad, adding in the remaining peas.

Marinated kipper fillets and tomato salad

Serves 4–5 Time taken: 20 minutes

2 198 g (7 oz) tins kipper fillets
4–5 firm medium-sized tomatoes
1 medium-sized onion, finely chopped
1 tablespoon capers
1 heaped tablespoon parsley, finely chopped
2–3 tablespoons wine vinegar

Drain the oil from the kippers, saving one teaspoonful. Arrange the kippers in a flat dish. Then cut the tomatoes into thin slices. Spread these over the kippers. Finely chop the onion, capers and parsley. Combine them with the vinegar and the kipper oil and pour over the kippers and tomatoes.

Cover the dish with silver foil and let it marinate for 10–15 minutes before serving.

Kipper mousse

Serves 4 Time taken: 5 minutes

1 198 g (7 oz) tin kipper fillets
1 50 ml (¼ pint) soured cream
squeeze of lemon and lemon slices

Drain the oil from the kippers and skin them. Then mash them in a bowl, mixing in a little lemon juice as you do so. Add soured cream and mix thoroughly. Fill ramekins with the mixture and serve individually, garnished with a slice of lemon. Put into the refrigerator to cool.

Kipper pâté

Serves 4–5 Time taken: 5 minutes

Kipper pâté is easy to make, inexpensive and very tasty. Kipper fillets in tins are of good enough quality to use for pâté.

2 198 g (7 oz) tins kipper fillets in edible oil
110 g (4 oz) soft butter
juice of 1 lemon
2 tablespoons parsley, very finely chopped
freshly milled black pepper
½ teaspoon mace

Drain all the oil from the kipper fillets, then put the fillets into a blender to produce a smooth pâté. (If you prefer a rougher texture mash with a fork instead.) Blend in the soft butter well, add lemon juice, the parsley, plenty of pepper and the mace. Mix well. Pack the pâté in a small pâté dish and put into the fridge to chill.

Serve with hot toast and additional slices of lemon.

Sardines in vinaigrette

Serves 4

Time taken: 15 minutes

- 1–2 garlic cloves, crushed
- 1 level teaspoon made-up mustard – French or English
- 3 tablespoons olive oil
- 1 tablespoon white wine vinegar
- salt and freshly ground black pepper
- 1 heaped tablespoon parsley, finely chopped
- 1 heaped tablespoon chives, finely chopped
- 2 125 g (4¾ oz) tins sardines in edible oil

In a small mixing bowl combine the garlic, mustard, oil, vinegar, salt and pepper and stir vigorously until a smooth and even dressing is obtained. Add the parsley and chives and mix well.

Drain off any excess oil from the sardines. Arrange them on a shallow or flat plate and pour the vinaigrette over.

Serve with thin slices of brown bread and butter.

Mackerel pâté

Serves 4

Time taken: 15 minutes

- 1 212 g (7½ oz) tin mackerel in tomato sauce
- 1 large hard-boiled egg
- 1 heaped tablespoon fresh parsley, finely chopped
- freshly milled black pepper
- ¼ teaspoon of ground mace
- 50 g (2 oz) butter, softened

Thoroughly drain the mackerel then put it into a bowl and mash with a fork. Chop the egg and add to the bowl, followed by the parsley, the pepper and the mace. Finally add the butter and continue mashing until the mixture turns pale and the ingredients have blended together into a smooth paste. Should you have some soured cream handy, a tablespoon of it would make this pâté even more delicious.

Salmon mousse

Serves 4

Preparation time: 15 minutes
Cooling time: 15–20 minutes

- 1 212 g (7½ oz) tin red salmon
- juice of ½ lemon
- salt and freshly milled black pepper
- 1 egg white
- 15 g (½ oz) powdered gelatine dissolved in 4 tablespoons very hot water
- 1 150 ml (5 fl oz) carton double cream
- lemon slices to garnish

Mash the salmon in a bowl with a fork removing any obvious bits of bone. Do not strive for a smooth texture as a few coarser flakes add to the taste. Mix in the lemon juice and season with salt and pepper. In a separate bowl beat the egg white until stiff and fold into the salmon. Now turn to the gelatine: sprinkle it on to very hot water in a cup and stir until it is well dissolved. If you have difficulty dissolving the gelatine stand the cup in a pan of warm water over a low heat. Thoroughly incorporate the gelatine into the fish mixture, then fold in the lightly whipped cream. Place the mousse into individual ramekins and garnish with lemon slices. Chill on the coldest shelf of your fridge until it sets – it shouldn't take longer than 15–20 minutes. Serve with hot toast.

Red salmon with mushrooms and vinaigrette

Serves 4

Time taken: 15 minutes

3 tablespoons olive oil
1 tablespoon wine vinegar
salt and freshly milled black pepper
115 g (4 oz) mushrooms, finely sliced
bunch of chives, finely chopped
1 142 ml (5 fl oz) carton double cream
3 tablespoons mayonnaise
1 212 g (7½ oz) tin red salmon

In a medium-sized bowl combine the olive oil and vinegar with the salt and pepper. Add the mushrooms and half the amount of chives and mix well. Put the mushrooms to one side to marinate.

In another small bowl whip the cream until thick but not stiff, add the mayonnaise and mix together thoroughly. Drain the salmon and flake it with a fork; then add to the marinated mushrooms. Put the prepared cream and mayonnaise in. Mix gently and taste to see if the salt and pepper seasoning is adequate. Add more if desired.

After a final very gentle mix put on to a shallow serving dish and sprinkle with the remaining chives.

Tuna fish with fresh coriander

Serves 4–5

Time taken: 15 minutes

115 g (4 oz) fresh coriander (to be found in Oriental shops)
1 medium head celery
1 large onion, chopped
2–3 garlic cloves
2 tablespoons oil
juice of 1 lemon
1–4 tablespoons water (or to taste)
salt and freshly milled black pepper
2 198 g (7 oz) tins tuna fish

Finely chop all the vegetables. Put the oil in a saucepan and fry the vegetables for 2–3 minutes. Add the lemon juice and the water and sprinkle with salt and pepper. Cook for 2–3 minutes. Add the tuna fish in large chunks, mix gently and simmer for another 2–3 minutes. This is delicious served hot and with bread.

To make this dish even tastier, a sliced green pepper and chopped parsley could be added to the vegetables.

Taramasalata

Serves 4 Time taken: 15 minutes

This is a very appetizing *hors d'oeuvre* and one which can be served on both formal and informal occasions or even as a dip to have with drinks. It can also be made in advance and kept in the fridge.

1 70 g (2½ oz) pot smoked cod's roe
1 garlic clove, sliced
200 ml (⅓ pint) oil
150 ml (¼ pint) milk
3½–4 tablespoons lemon juice
2½ large pieces sliced bread without crusts soaked in 2–3 tablespoons milk
a little pepper
teaspoon chopped parsley to garnish

Put the smoked cod's roe together with the garlic into the blender. Measure out the right quantities of oil, milk and lemon juice and set aside. Break up the bread with your hands and put it in a bowl to soak in the milk. Now add it to the liquidizer together with some of the prepared milk and oil and switch on for a few seconds. Gradually incorporate (while the blender is still on) all the milk, the oil, as well as the lemon juice, into the cod's roe mixture. Season with a little pepper. The mixture should now be smooth and creamy and have the consistency of mayonnaise. Should it not be thick enough add a little more oil. Place in a serving dish, garnish with the parsley and chill until ready to serve. Serve with hot toast or pitta (oriental bread).

Tahina

Serves 6–8 Time taken: 15 minutes

Tahina is a purée of pure sesame seed and is very common in Eastern Mediterranean countries. It is easy to prepare. Tahina can be served as an appetizer with pitta (oriental bread) or as a sauce with fish and fresh or cooked vegetables.

1 425 g (15 oz) jar tahina
150 ml (¼ pint) water
juice of 1 very large or two small lemons
3–4 crushed garlic cloves
salt and freshly ground black pepper

If the tahina has stood for a long time the seed sinks to the bottom and clear oil rises to the top of the jar. The first step then is to tip the contents into a bowl and mix thoroughly together so that they combine into one. Pour in the water very gradually, stirring all the time. When the mixture is smooth and even, add the lemon juice, garlic, salt and pepper to taste. Mix well and serve in individual dishes or in a communal serving dish for people to dip into.

Chick pea dip

Serves 4–5 Time taken: 15 minutes

Tinned chick peas make this popular Greek dish easy to prepare. There is no longer any need to soak fresh chick peas overnight – the tinned product is instant and excellent.

1 397 g (14 oz) tin chick peas
4 tablespoons olive oil
3 tablespoons lemon juice
2–3 garlic cloves, crushed
salt
1 pickled cucumber, very finely chopped
1 pickled pimento, finely chopped

Drain the chick peas and save the liquid as you may need some of it at a later stage.

Put the chick peas into a mixing bowl and mash with a fork until they blend into a paste, but don't overdo it as the slightly rough texture is very pleasant. As you work 3 tablespoons of oil in, add the lemon juice, garlic and salt. If the mixture is too thick for your liking add a little of the chick pea liquid to dilute the mixture. When it is well blended put the purée on to a serving dish or into individual dishes. Make a well in the centre, pour in the last tablespoon of oil and fill with the chopped pickled cucumber and pimento.

Hoummous

Serves 5 Time taken: 10 minutes

This recipe for hoummous is very quickly got together and different from the previous recipe which has a rougher texture. It requires little work but the additional ingredients will make a world of difference.

1 425 g (15 oz) tin hoummous
2 garlic cloves, crushed
juice of 1½ lemons
1 heaped tablespoon fresh parsley, chopped
2 tablespoons (approximately) olive oil
sprinkling of paprika (optional)
pitta (oriental bread)

Tip the hoummous into a bowl, add the crushed garlic and mix well. Stir in the lemon juice followed by one tablespoon of oil. Divide the mixture into individual portions or tip it into a serving dish. Add the other tablespoon of oil but do not mix it in – swirl it over the hoummous. Garnish with the chopped parsley and a sprinkle of paprika if desired. Cool in the fridge for a while before serving with hot pitta.

Aubergine dip

Serves 4–5 Time taken: 10 minutes

Here is a suggestion for a very tasty *hors d'oeuvre* using tinned aubergine slices.

1 369 g (13 oz) tin fried aubergine slices
1 150 ml (¼ pint) carton natural yogurt
a little salt
lemon slices
chopped parsley to garnish

Keep two dessertspoons of the oil from the tin of aubergines and throw away the rest. Now put the aubergines and the oil in a mixing bowl and mash very thoroughly with a fork until the mixture is smooth. Add 3 dessertspoons of yogurt, a pinch of salt and mix well. Tip into a serving bowl or spoon out the mixture on to individual small plates. Spread a little yogurt on each portion and cut a thickish slice of lemon in half for each person and place in the centre of the mixture – lemon juice does wonders for this recipe. Sprinkle generously with parsley and chill before serving. Serve with hot toast – this is a rich *hors d'oeuvre* and needs lots of it.

Main courses

The main course of a meal is often associated in people minds with the rituals of roasting, serving, carving and carving again. Although people are only too glad to resort to tins for snacks, accompaniments or desserts, they will shy away from using tinned food for a main dish. Of course just to open a tin of beef or pork and present it as it comes, would indeed be dull. It's what you do with it that counts – more so with the main dish than with any other, for the main dish is after all the highlight of a meal. You may be giving your carving knife or skewers a rest but your meal needn't be any the worse for it. And if you are in a hurry the gains will certainly outweigh the losses.

In this section you will find ways of making a variety of dishes ranging from the traditional 'Fisherman's Pie' and 'Beef with Tomatoes and Mushrooms', to the more adventurous 'Pork and Aubergine in Garlic Sauce' or 'Chicken with Peaches and Wine'. A number of more exotic and spicy dishes such as 'Chilli Con Carne' and 'Ham Curry with Pineapple' are also included. From time to time we have suggested ways of making your own sauce and of course a variety of different additional ingredients are suggested throughout.

For easy reference, we have divided this section into five main parts – Beef, Pork, Chicken, Fish and rounding off with a small 'Odd-tin-out' section which includes pasta dishes and omelettes.

Beef

Beef paprika

Serves 2–3

Time taken: 15 minutes

This recipe is a lovely rich red colour and looks very attractive. It can be prepared within minutes and would, without a doubt, impress your unexpected guest.

2 medium onions
3 tablespoons oil
1 heaped teaspoon paprika
1 heaped dessertspoon tomato purée (tinned or in a tube)
1 tablespoon flour
For the stock: ¼ beef cube dissolved in 150 ml (¼ pint) boiling water

1 440 g (15½ oz) tin chunky beef
1 clove garlic, crushed
salt and freshly milled black pepper
1 small green pepper
1 tablespoon soured cream

Peel and thinly slice the onions and gently fry them in the heated oil until soft. Stir in the paprika first, then add the tomato purée, the tablespoon of flour and the stock. Go on stirring for about 2–3 minutes. Open the tin of meat and tip its contents into the pan, followed by the crushed garlic and the salt and pepper. Simmer for 5 minutes or until the meat is hot. Wash the pepper, remove the seeds and cut it into small strips. Add to the pan and gently bring to the boil. The pepper in this recipe should not be overcooked. Stir in the soured cream at the last minute and serve with plain boiled rice.

Spicy beef

Serves 2–3

Time taken: 20 minutes

1 small onion
1 garlic clove
knob of butter
¼ teaspoon powdered ginger
¼ teaspoon powdered turmeric
¼ teaspoon powdered chilli
2 fresh tomatoes (put in boiling water first for easy peeling)
1 440 g (15½ oz) tin chunky beef
juice of ½ lemon
salt and freshly milled black pepper

Finely chop the onion and garlic and gently fry in the hot butter until soft. Add the ginger, turmeric and chilli to the pan and fry for 2–3 minutes stirring all the time. Remove the skin from the tomatoes and chop them up, put them in the pan and stir for a few minutes. Tip the chunky beef in, together with the lemon juice as well as some salt and pepper. Do not over-season as this dish is quite spicy already. Simmer for 10 minutes with the lid on, stirring every now and then. Serve on a bed of rice.

Sultana and banana beef curry

Serves 2–3

Time taken: 25 minutes

This curry can be made fairly hot as the banana and the sultanas will help to cool things down. Since curry powders vary a lot, test a little first before you use it and adjust the quantity accordingly.

1 onion, thinly sliced
1 garlic clove, thinly sliced
large knob butter
¾ teaspoon curry powder
½ teaspoon turmeric
6 tablespoons boiling water
1 425 g (15 oz) tin chunky beef
3 tomatoes, peeled and chopped (put in boiling water first for easy peeling)
3 dessertspoons sultanas (put in boiling water first to soften)
1 large banana
salt and freshly milled black pepper

Soften the onion and garlic in the hot butter. Add the curry powder and the turmeric and stir for a few minutes, then gradually pour in the boiling water and continue stirring until the ingredients have blended. Add the beef, followed by the chopped tomatoes and the sultanas, and simmer for 10 minutes to allow the spices to penetrate the meat. Slice the banana into thickish rounds, then add to the pan and season according to taste. Cook on a low heat for 5–7 minutes, but no longer or else the banana will disintegrate.

Beef, prune and celery pie

Serves 4–5

Preparation time: 10 minutes
Baking time: 30 minutes

This substantial dish is quick to prepare but takes a little while to bake, so have a starter at the ready.

1 440 g (15½ oz) tin chunky beef
2 teaspoons paprika
1 tablespoon tomato purée
6 tablespoons hot water (approximately)
2½ teaspoons dried tarragon
12 dried prunes (softened in boiling water)
salt and freshly milled pepper
1 524 g (1 lb 2½ oz) tin celery hearts
1 154 g (5½ oz) packet instant mashed potato
butter
1 generous tablespoon Parmesan cheese

Empty the tin of meat into an ovenproof dish. In a small bowl blend the paprika and the tomato purée with the hot water and pour into the dish. Adjust the quantity of water if necessary – it will depend on the brand of chunky meat used, if it contains a lot of gravy you will need less water. Sprinkle the tarragon over the meat. Cut the prunes in half and stone them. Place them in the dish and season with salt and pepper. Then give all the ingredients a good stir with a wooden spoon. Spread the mixture evenly in the dish and arrange the drained celery on top.

Preheat oven to 180°C, 350°F or Gas No. 4.

Make the mashed potato according to the instructions on the packet, but use only half water and the other half milk – this improves the texture. While it's still hot add a knob of butter, salt and pepper to taste and mix well. Now spread the potato over the celery and top with additional pieces of butter and a generous sprinkling of Parmesan cheese. Bake for 30 minutes and serve with a crisp lettuce salad.

Beef casserole with green pepper

Serves 3–4

Time taken: 20 minutes

This lovely stew is very quickly got together and can be served with either rice or pasta.

4 tablespoons oil
1 medium onion, finely chopped
1 clove garlic, crushed
2 bay leaves
1 425 g (15 oz) tin tomatoes
1 440 g (15½ oz) tin chunky beef
1 green pepper
3 tablespoons cooking wine
salt and freshly milled black pepper

Heat the oil in a saucepan and gently fry the onion, the garlic and the bay leaves. Empty the contents of the tin of tomatoes into the saucepan and mash them up with a fork. Cook for 5 minutes, then add the chunky beef, the roughly chopped pepper as well as the wine, salt and pepper. Simmer for at least 10 minutes so that the ingredients are well blended and a nice flavour is obtained. Do not worry if the pepper is not cooked through; it's much nicer if it's crisp and firm.

Stuffed cabbage leaves with meat and creamy sauce

Serves 10–12

Preparation time: 40 minutes
Baking time: approximately 1 hour

Cabbage leaves can be stuffed with a variety of fillings and a large cabbage yielding 25 or so leaves is ideal for a dinner party. Here is a meat filling you might like to try. (See p. 103 for a vegetable filling.)

For the filling:
1 large onion, sliced
2 cloves garlic, crushed
2–3 tablespoons oil
1 440 g (15½ oz) tin minced beef
2 tablespoons tomato purée
pinch of dried herbs
salt and freshly milled black pepper
1 large green cabbage (900–1350 g 2–3 lbs)

For the sauce:
knob of butter
3½–4 tablespoons flour
750 ml (1¼ pint) milk
pinch of nutmeg
50 g (2 oz) grated cheese
salt and freshly milled black pepper
1 generous tablespoon Parmesan cheese

Begin by making the filling. Fry the onion and garlic in the hot oil for a few minutes than add the minced beef, tomato purée, herbs and the salt and pepper. Tinned meat varies a lot from brand to brand so taste a little before you season it.

Wash the cabbage, remove the damaged outer leaves then boil the rest whole in a large pan of salted water for 8–15 minutes or until tender, and drain in a colander. Do not throw away the water as you may need it again. Swill cold water over the cabbage or it will be too hot to handle. Pull the cabbage leaves off one at a time and snip off part of the stalks for easier rolling – return the cabbage to the boil if the inner leaves still seem a little hard. Place a dessertspoon of meat into the centre of each leaf, tuck the sides in and roll them up; you should have enough stuffing for 25. Pack the rolled cabbage leaves close together in an ovenproof dish and sprinkle with salt and pepper.

Preheat oven to 180°C, 350°F or Gas No. 4.

Now make a light cheese sauce by melting the butter in a pan. Gradually add the flour and milk and stir constantly to avoid lumps. When it has thickened just a bit, add the nutmeg, grated cheese and salt and pepper. Pour the sauce over the cabbage, sprinkle with Parmesan cheese and nutmeg, cover with foil and cook for 1–1¼ hours. Take the foil off for the last 10 minutes or so and allow the top to brown.

Minced meat with cabbage leaves and pineapple

Serves 4

Time taken: 35 minutes

1 440 g (15½ oz) tin pineapple slices
5–6 fresh white cabbage leaves
salt and freshly milled black pepper
¼ teaspoon paprika
¼ teaspoon marjoram
1 425 g (15 oz) tin minced beef

Drain off the juice from the pineapple and put half into a saucepan (the rest is not used in this recipe). Cut the pineapple slices in half. Trim the cabbage leaves and tear each one into largish pieces of an irregular shape (this is much nicer than cutting them up with a knife). Put them into the saucepan and add the salt, pepper, paprika and marjoram. Bring to the boil and cook on a low heat for 15 minutes or until the cabbage leaves are soft.

Preheat the oven to 190°C, 375°F or Gas No. 5.

Drain the cabbage leaves and arrange half in an ovenproof dish. Spread half the minced beef on top followed by the pineapple, then the rest of the meat and cover with remaining cabbage leaves. Bake in the oven for 15 minutes.

Chilli con carne

Serves 3–4

Time taken: 15 minutes

3 tablespoons oil
2 onions, chopped
1 clove garlic, finely chopped
½ teaspoon chilli powder
1 heaped tablespoon tomato purée
3 tablespoons boiling water
1 440 g (15½ oz) tin minced beef
1 284 g (10 oz) tin red kidney beans
salt and freshly milled black pepper

Heat the oil in a pan and fry the onion and garlic until soft. Before adding the chilli powder, test its strength as chilli powders vary a great deal, though this dish should be eaten fairly hot.

Now add the chilli powder, tomato purée and boiling water and mix well with a wooden spoon. Empty the contents of the tin of mince into the pan and stir for a few minutes. Thoroughly drain the red kidney beans and add to the other ingredients, then season to taste. Give the mixture a good stir and leave on until hot, but do not overcook as tinned mince is already quite soft.

Cannelloni with minced beef in curry sauce

Serves 4–6 | Time taken: 35 minutes

1 376 g (13¼ oz) tin curry sauce
1 425 g (15 oz) tin minced beef in rich gravy
12 cannelloni from a 250 g (8¾ oz) packet

Preheat the oven to 220°C, 425°F or Gas No. 7.
Pour the curry sauce into a small bowl. Press the minced beef down in the tin with a wooden spoon and drain the excess liquid into the curry sauce.

Using a small spoon fill the cannelloni with the mince. Arrange them next to each other in a shallow ovenproof dish, one that is just large enough to accommodate the cannelloni and the sauce: don't let them overlap or they'll stick together during the cooking. Give the curry sauce a good stir and pour it over the cannelloni. Bake in the oven for 25 minutes.

Meat and lady's fingers crumble

Serves 4–6
Preparation time: 15 minutes
Baking time: 30 minutes

This is a hot and exotic dish, unusual in texture, which will impress your family or guests. Served with a selection of green salads and a few boiled potatoes, it is ideal for lunch.

115 g (4 oz) margarine
227 g (8 oz) self-raising flour
425 g (15 oz) tin minced beef in rich gravy
400 g (14 oz) tin lady's fingers (okra)
1 tablespoon parsley, finely chopped
½ teaspoon celery salt
crushed chillies to taste (from a jar)
1 meat cube dissolved in 300 ml (½ pint) boiling water
142 g (5 oz) tin tomato purée
1 medium onion, finely chopped

Begin by making the crumble in a bowl: rub the margarine and flour together with your finger tips. Add a little salt and put aside.

Preheat oven to 180°C, 350°F or Gas No. 4.

Put half the amount of mince into a deep medium-sized ovenproof dish, spreading it evenly across the bottom. Drain the lady's fingers and put half of them over the meat. Taste to see whether more salt and pepper is required as tins of lady's fingers tend to vary from manufacturer to manufacturer. Sprinkle over the parsley, add the celery salt and crushed chillies to taste. Build up a second layer in the same way with meat, lady's fingers and seasoning. Add the tomato purée to the hot stock in a bowl, and mix thoroughly. Add the onion, more crushed chillies if desired and a little salt. Mix once more and pour over the prepared ingredients in the dish. Prick with a fork several times to allow the liquid to seep through. Sprinkle the crumble over the top and bake for 30 minutes.

Roly poly minced beef

Serves 4–6

Preparation time: 15 minutes
Baking time: 25 minutes

1 454 g (1 lb) packet short pastry
1 large onion, finely chopped
3 tablespoons oil
1 teaspoon ground celery seed
115 g (4 oz) mushrooms, sliced
1 425 g (15 oz) tin minced beef

It is probably easier to make two small roly polies than one big one, so start by cutting the pastry into two even pieces. On a floured surface, roll out the pastry, then cut it into two roughly equal portions and put aside for a while.

Preheat oven to 190°C, 375°F or Gas No. 5.

In a small pan fry the onion in the heated oil until soft, then add the celery seed, sliced mushrooms and minced meat. Mix well and cook for 1–2 minutes. Take half the mixture, spread it evenly over the pastry and roll it up into a long sausage. Prick the pastry with a fork to allow air to get through. Now make the second roly poly with the rest of the mixture and bake for 25 minutes.

Cottage pie

Serves 4

Preparation time: 15 minutes
Baking time: 45 minutes

1 small onion, finely chopped
3 tablespoons oil
1 425 g (15 oz) tin minced beef
pinch dried herbs
2 tablespoons Worcestershire sauce
salt and freshly milled black pepper
1 397 g (14 oz) tin tomatoes
1 154 g (5½ oz) packet instant mashed potato
knob of butter
50 g (2 oz) grated cheese
sprinkle of Parmesan cheese

Fry the onion in the heated oil until soft. Add the beef, the dried herbs and the Worcestershire sauce and stir for 5 minutes. Season to taste. Butter a deep ovenproof dish and tip the mixture into it. Drain the tomatoes thoroughly and arrange them on top of the beef.

Turn oven on to 180°C, 350°F or Gas No. 4.

Make the instant mashed potato according to the directions on the packet and stir in the butter, grated cheese and some freshly milled pepper. Place the mash over the tomatoes, sprinkle Parmesan cheese over the top and bake for 45 minutes.

Moussaka

Serves 4

Preparation time: 20 minutes
Cooking time: 45 minutes

Moussaka as made by the Greeks uses cooked lamb but minced beef makes a good substitute.

1 finely chopped small onion
4 tablespoons oil
1 425 g (15 oz) tin of minced beef
1 clove garlic, crushed
2 tablespoons tomato purée (from a tin or tube)
pinch of cinnamon
50 g (2 oz) grated cheese or Parmesan
1 large aubergine

For the sauce:
knob of butter
2 tablespoons flour
300 ml (½ pint) milk
salt and freshly milled black pepper
pinch of nutmeg
1 egg

Fry the onion until soft in half the oil. Empty the contents of the tin of beef into a mixing bowl and add the fried onion, garlic, tomato purée and the cinnamon. Mix the ingredients thoroughly with a wooden spoon and place in a greased ovenproof dish. Sprinkle half the amount of grated cheese over the top and keep the rest aside for later.

Wash and cut the aubergine into thinnish slices. Heat the remaining oil and lightly fry the slices in it. You may need a little more oil as aubergines soak it up quickly. Drain on absorbent paper and arrange the slices over the meat.

Turn oven on to 180°C, 350°F or Gas No. 4.

Melt the butter for the sauce over a low heat, stir in the flour and gradually add the milk. When the sauce has thickened, season with salt and pepper as well as the nutmeg and draw off the heat. Allow to cool for 2–3 minutes. Whisk the egg in a separate bowl, add it to the sauce and then pour over the meat and aubergine. Sprinkle the remaining cheese over the top and bake for 45 minutes.

Minced beef with tomatoes and mushrooms

Serves 4–5

Time taken: 15 minutes

- 3 tablespoons oil
- 1 large onion, finely chopped
- 1 425 g (15 oz) tin Scotch minced beef
- 1 300 g (10½ oz) tin tomato and mushroom spaghetti sauce
- 1 clove garlic, finely chopped
- chopped parsley
- salt and freshly milled black pepper

Melt the oil in a saucepan and fry the onion until soft. Skim the fat from the minced beef, put the meat into the saucepan and cook for 2–3 minutes. Add the tomato and mushroom sauce, the garlic and parsley as well as salt and plenty of pepper. Mix well and simmer for about 5 minutes.

Jellied meat balls with cucumber

Serves 3–4

Preparation time: 7 minutes
Setting time: 30 minutes

This is a dish to serve cold. Try it for lunch on warm days with a fresh green salad.

- 1 425 g (15 oz) tin meat balls in brown sauce
- ¼ of a fresh large cucumber, chopped into squares
- 1 largish pickled cucumber, finely chopped
- freshly milled black pepper
- 1 sachet aspic jelly
- 150 ml (¼ pint) of hot, not boiling water

Take the meatballs out of the tin and place into a small bowl: the gravy should be left in the tin for the time being. Add both kinds of cucumber to the bowl and season well with black pepper.

Dissolve the aspic in the water and add the gravy from the tin to make up to 300 ml (½ pint) of liquid. (If it does not equal that amount add a little more water.) Mix thoroughly and pour over the meat balls and cucumber in the bowl. Give a final gentle mix to all the ingredients taking care not to break the meatballs.

Put the bowl in the refrigerator to cool and set.

Meat balls with cabbage

Serves 2–3

Time taken: 25 minutes

425 g (15 oz) tin meatballs in brown gravy
340 g (12 oz) fresh white cabbage, finely shredded
3 tablespoons oil
2 tablespoons soya sauce
1 tablespoon sherry
1 tablespoon cornflour dissolved in 2 tablespoons water
salt and freshly milled black pepper

If you have not used tinned meat balls before, open the tin and check the amount of gravy it contains because this will determine how much water will be needed later.

Heat the oil in a saucepan, and fry the cabbage and celery on a high heat for 2–3 minutes, stirring with a wooden spatula. Switch off the heat. Pour in the soya sauce and sherry and slowly blend in the dissolved cornflour. Season with salt and pepper, mix well and reheat to boiling point. If the tin of meatballs contains too little gravy, add a little water to the vegetables now. Tip the contents into the saucepan, stirring very gently and then arrange the meatballs on top of the vegetables. Cover with a tight lid and cook for ten minutes. Serve hot with mashed or boiled potatoes.

Corned beef, potato and lettuce salad

Serves 4–5

Time taken: 15–20 minutes

1 340 g (12 oz) tin corned beef
several lettuce leaves
1 540 g (1 lb 3 oz) tin new potatoes
3 celery sticks
1 green pepper
40 g (1½ oz) broken walnuts

For the dressing:
4 tablespoons oil
2 tablespoons vinegar
2 teaspoons fresh tarragon
1 tablespoon mayonnaise
salt and freshly milled black pepper

Before you start preparing this salad, put the corned beef in the fridge as it will be easier to slice.

Have a medium-sized platter ready, wash enough lettuce to go round the edge and let the lettuce dry while you get the rest of the ingredients together. Thoroughly drain the new potatoes. Wash the celery and the pepper and cut them into smallish pieces roughly the same size as the potatoes. Add them to the potatoes together with the walnuts. Mix well.

In a separate bowl, put the oil, vinegar and tarragon and beat with a fork. Now add the mayonnaise, stirring vigorously until it is well blended and until the dressing is opaque and creamy. Season with salt and pepper to taste. Pour over the vegetables (reserving about 1 tablespoon for the lettuce) and mix until the dressing has been soaked up.

Arrange the lettuce round the platter and put the vegetables in the middle. Pour some of the remaining dressing on the lettuce and arrange the corned beef slices over it.

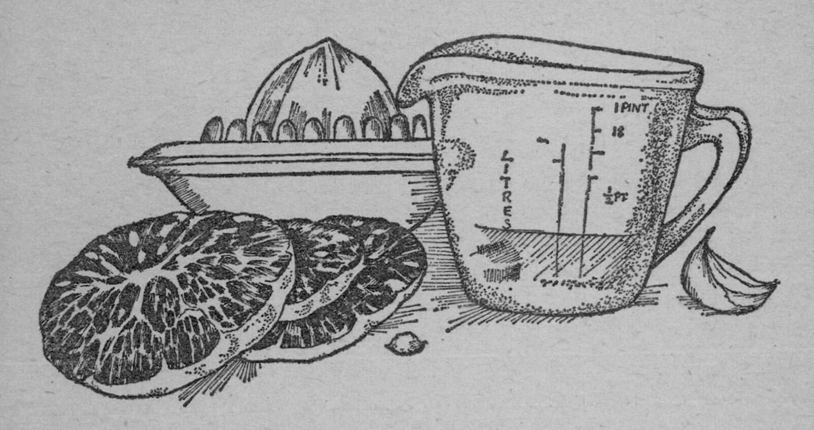

Pork

Pork with orange

Serves 4

Time taken: 25 minutes

knob of butter
1 large onion, sliced
2 large garlic cloves, sliced
For the stock: 1 chicken cube dissolved in 150 ml (¼ pint) boiling water
juice of 1 orange
1 teaspoon soft brown sugar
salt and freshly milled black pepper
1 tablespoon parsley, chopped
squeeze of lemon (optional)
1 300 g (10½ oz) tin pork in natural juice
1 orange

Melt the butter in a saucepan and gently fry the onion and garlic until golden brown. Gradually pour in the stock, stirring all the time, then add the juice of one orange as well as some of the pulp as this adds to the flavour. Stir in the sugar, season with salt and plenty of black pepper and sprinkle the parsley on. Mix well for about two minutes and add the lemon. The latter is optional and need only be used if a sharper taste is required.

Take the pork out of tin and remove all excess fat or jelly. Cut the pork into four even slices and put in the saucepan. Now peel and slice the orange and lay above the pork in the saucepan. Spoon the sauce over the pork several times, cover the pan with a tight lid and simmer for 5–7 minutes. Serve with rice or potato.

Pork and aubergine in garlic sauce

Serves 4

Time taken: 15 minutes

2–3 garlic cloves, sliced
3 tablespoons cooking oil
1 70 g (2½ oz) tin tomato purée
300 ml (½ pint) water
¼ teaspoon dry marjoram
1 300 g (10½ oz) tin pork
1 396 g (14 oz) tin stuffed aubergine

Slice the garlic and fry it in the oil until golden brown. Reduce the heat and pour in the tomato purée and water a little at a time, stirring constantly. Add the marjoram.

Cut the pork into small pieces (you should have about 20 to 30 pieces), put into the saucepan and mix thoroughly but gently. Arrange the aubergine over the pork and spoon the sauce over it from time to time. Cook for 7–10 minutes with the lid firmly on.

Pork with aubergines and lima beans

Serves 4–5

Time taken: 25 minutes

1 454 g (1 lb) tin lima beans, drained
2 garlic cloves, crushed
1 heaped tablespoon fresh parsley, finely chopped
salt and freshly milled black pepper
1 454 g (1 lb) tin pork shoulder, sweet cured
1 370 g (14 oz) tin stuffed aubergine slices

Preheat oven to 220°C, 425°F or Gas No. 7.
Place the beans, garlic and parsley in a medium-sized casserole dish, and season with a little salt and plenty of pepper. Mix thoroughly and put aside.

Now open the tin of pork at both ends so that its contents come out more easily. Put the pork on a wooden board and cut into thin slices. Open the tin of aubergines and alternate layers of pork and aubergines on the lima beans, finishing with a layer of aubergines.

No additional seasoning is necessary as both the pork and the aubergines are very rich.

Cover the casserole dish with a tight lid and put into the oven for 15–20 minutes. Serve hot with rice or potatoes.

Pork in wine with nuts

Serves 4 — Time taken: 30 minutes

Don't be put off by the long list of ingredients! To prepare this dish quickly, start by chopping and slicing all the vegetables first, so that they are ready when required.

3 tablespoons oil
1 small onion, finely sliced
1 carrot, finely sliced
1 celery stick, finely sliced
1 tablespoon flour
1 chicken cube dissolved in 450 ml (¾ pint) boiling water
freshly milled black pepper
1 heaped teaspoon tomato purée
pinch of thyme
pinch of mace
pinch of marjoram
5 medium-sized mushrooms with stalks, sliced
1 tablespoon parsley, finely chopped
a handful of walnuts
50 g (2 oz) raisins (soak in boiling water first to soften)
5 tablespoons red wine or port
1 454 (1 lb) tin chopped ham with pork

Preheat the oven to mark 180°C, 350°F or Gas No. 4.
Heat the oil in a medium-sized pan and gently fry the onion, carrot and celery for 4–5 minutes. Reduce the heat, mix in the flour and stir for a little while until the flour is well blended. Now gradually pour in about a third of the stock, carry on stirring and pour in another third. Season well with pepper, add the tomato purée, herbs and then the remaining stock. Add the mushrooms, parsley, nuts and raisins (drained of their water). Simmer for a few minutes, stir and pour in the wine. Leave on a low heat for a few minutes and put aside.

Cut the ham into approximately 1 cm (½ in) strips and place in a shallow oven dish. Pour the prepared sauce over the ham, cover with foil and cook in the oven for 10 minutes. The sauce in this recipe is rich and delicious. Serve with plain boiled rice or instant mashed potato.

Sweet and sour pork

Serves 2–3 Time taken: 20 minutes

Try this Chinese dish and don't be put off by the long list of ingredients as you will find most of them in your store cupboard or larder anyway.

For the sauce:
1 tablespoon sugar
1 tablespoon orange juice
1 tablespoon vinegar
1 tablespoon tomato purée
1 tablespoon soya sauce
1 tablespoon sherry
½ tablespoon cornflour dissolved in 2 tablespoons water
few drops chilli sauce (tabasco)
1 tablespoon pickles
1 tablespoon oil

1 454 g (1 lb) tin cooked ham
1 level tablespoon cornflour
4 tablespoons oil
1 red or green pepper

Prepare the sauce first by mixing all the ingredients except the pickles and oil in a bowl. Heat the oil and fry the chopped pickles in it for a minute, then pour the prepared sauce into it. Cook until it thickens and put aside for later.

Open the tin of ham and remove all the jelly, Cut the ham into 2 cm (¾ in) cubes and lightly dust on all sides with the cornflour. Heat 3 tablespoons of oil in a frying pan and brown the pieces of ham in it, turning them over so that all sides get done. Do not fry them for too long as they may fall apart. While these are on, quickly wash and cut the pepper into thin 5 cm (2 in) long strips – then fry the strips in a separate pan on a high heat in 1 tablespoon of oil and add the sweet and sour sauce, stirring until it has thickened. Add the fried pieces of ham and cook for a minute or so. Stir so that all the pieces of ham get thoroughly covered with the sauce. Serve straight away.

Cold pork and lima bean salad

Serves 4–6 Time taken: 15 minutes

This well-flavoured salad is very substantial and will make a meal on its own. You can feed a family in no time at all.

- 1 454 g (1 lb) fancy small green lima beans, drained
- 2 garlic cloves, finely chopped
- 1 teaspoon dry mustard
- salt and freshly milled black pepper

For French dressing:

- 5 tablespoons olive oil
- 2 tablespoons wine vinegar
- salt and freshly milled black pepper
- 3 spring onions, finely chopped
- 2 tablespoons shredded cheddar cheese
- 1 454 g (1 lb) tin sweet cured pork shoulder
- 1–2 lettuce hearts

Mix the beans with the crushed garlic, mustard, salt and pepper. Make the French dressing by stirring together vigorously the oil, vinegar, salt and pepper, and then pour over the lima beans. Add the onions and cheese and mix gently together with the beans.

Open the tin of pork at both ends – that way the contents will come out more easily. Place on a wooden board and slice the pork into thin strips. Add to the salad and toss.

Line a serving dish with lettuce leaves and spoon the salad out on top. Serve with thin slices of bread and butter.

Ham with mandarins

Serves 2–3 Time taken: 15 minutes

Undercooked onions with mandarins, in a peppery sauce, combine very well with ham.

- 312 g (11 oz) tin mandarins in syrup
- 1 heaped teaspoon cornflour
- 1 small onion, finely chopped
- 198 g (7 oz) tin ham
- salt and freshly milled black pepper

Put the contents of the tin of mandarins through a large sieve on top of a medium-sized saucepan to drain. Place the mandarin segments to one side.

Now add the cornflour to the syrup in the saucepan and mix thoroughly, making sure all the lumps are dissolved. Cook on a very low heat until the mixture changes colour and thickens. Take off the heat. Season well and mix. Add the mandarins, the chopped onion and sliced ham, including any gelatine or fat from around the sides of the ham tin. Mix gently and cook for 2–3 minutes.

Ham with mushrooms and peanuts in cranberry sauce

Serves 4 — Time taken: 15 minutes

1 454 g (1 lb) tin Danish ham
198 g (7 oz) cranberry sauce
a handful of salted peanuts
pinch of salt
pinch of mixed herbs
freshly milled black pepper
150 ml (¼ pint) hot water
115 g (4 oz) fresh mushrooms (or tinned), finely chopped

Turn the piece of ham on its side and cut it into four even slices. Place them in a shallow oven dish and put aside.

Preheat oven to 180°C, 350°F or Gas No. 4.

Put the cranberry sauce, peanuts, salt, herbs and the pepper into a small pan, place on a low heat, pour in the water gradually, and keep on stirring. Gently bring to the boil, add the sliced mushrooms and cook for 2–3 minutes. Before pouring the sauce over the ham, prick the slices with a fork so that the sauce penetrates right through. Cover with silver foil and bake for 10 minutes in the hot oven.

This dish is delicious served with either plain boiled rice or instant mashed potato from a packet.

Ham curry with pineapple

Serves 3 — Time taken: 20 minutes

50 g (2 oz) butter
1 onion, finely chopped
2 tablespoons curry powder
1 heaped tablespoon flour
450 ml (¾ pint) light stock
1 454 g (1 lb) tin cooked ham
1 432 g (15¼ oz) tin pineapple pieces
salt and freshly milled pepper (optional)

How successful your curry is will depend a lot on what curry powder you use. There is a large selection of brands on the market and it will be up to you to find the one you like best. Whatever brand you decide on, do make sure to test the strength of the curry powder before you use it. Don't simply follow the instructions on the tin.

Melt the butter in a saucepan and, when hot, fry the onion in it for a few minutes. Then stir in the curry powder. When it is well blended, add the flour a little at a time while gradually pouring in the stock. Keep on stirring to avoid lumps. Next, open the tin of ham and remove all the jelly, then cut it into small cubes. When the sauce has thickened put in the pieces of ham, cook for five minutes or so and add the drained pineapple. Taste the curry before you add the salt and pepper and season accordingly. Tinned ham is already quite salty and you may not need any more salt. Simmer for 10 minutes or more.

Sausages, baked beans and mash

Serves 5–6 | Time taken: 15 minutes

1 154 g (5½ oz) packet instant mashed potato
generous knob of butter
1 227 g (8 oz) tin hot dog sausages or any other kind
1 447 g (15¾ oz) tin baked beans
salt and freshly milled black pepper

Set the oven to 200°C, 400°F or Gas No. 6.
Make the mashed potato according to the instructions on the packet but use half water, half milk for the liquid as this will make the mash creamier. When the potato is ready stir in the knob of butter and season with salt and pepper. Drain the sausages and split them lengthways down the middle. Put the mash in a deep ovenproof dish and place the halved sausages over the mash, followed by the contents of the tin of baked beans. Bake for 10–15 minutes or until hot.

Sausages with aubergines

Serves 4–6 | Time taken: 20 minutes

This is ideal for a snack lunch. Serve with a green salad or even baked beans.

1 400 g (14 oz) stuffed aubergines
1 311 g (11 oz) beef or pork sausages

This dish is virtually ready to serve and will require very little work. The aubergines are already prepared with tomatoes, garlic and parsley and are very tasty.

Preheat oven to 180°C, 350°F or Gas No. 4.

Take the sausages out of the tin and remove fat if there is any. Then cut them in half lengthwise and place them in a small and shallow oven dish. Cover with the aubergines, making sure that there is a little aubergine between the sausages. Cover with foil and bake in the oven for 10–15 minutes.

Toad in the hole

Serves 4

Preparation time: 15 minutes
Baking time: 45 minutes

140 g (5 oz) flour
pinch of salt
1 egg
300 ml (½ pint) milk and water mixed (¾ milk/¼ water)
freshly milled black pepper
pinch of mixed herbs
1–2 tablespoons oil
1 227 g (8 oz) tin frankfurters (or 8 sausages)

Preheat oven to 200°C, 400°F or Gas No. 6.

Begin by preparing the batter: sift the flour and the salt into a mixing bowl, then make a well in the centre and pour in the egg. Stir in half the milk and water, gradually drawing in the flour, and beating vigorously to avoid lumps. Add the remaining liquid, continuing to beat until the batter is smooth. Season with pepper and add the herbs.

Find an ovenproof dish large enough to accommodate the batter – an oblong or square one rather than a round one as the sausages will need spreading out. Put the oil in the dish and swirl it round, then heat for a few minutes in the hot oven. Fry the drained sausages for a few minutes, then pour the batter in. Bake for 40–45 minutes or until brown.

Sausages with sauerkraut, olives and cider

Serves 3–4

Time taken: 20 minutes

This snack dish is mild and pleasant in taste and would go very well with garlic bread.

1 420 g (14¾ oz) tin sauerkraut
4–5 tablespoons oil
2 dessertspoons black olives, stoned and finely chopped
300 ml (½ pint) strong dry cider
salt and freshly milled black pepper
1 227 g (8 oz) tin hot dogs in brine

Toss the sauerkraut in the hot oil for a few minutes. Add the olives, the cider, and the salt and pepper. Cook for 5–10 minutes, then add the drained sausages. Mix well so that the sausages absorb the cider and cook for 10 minutes. Arrange in a serving dish, with the sausages over the sauerkraut.

Sausages with grapes in white wine sauce

Serves 3–4 Time taken: 20 minutes

This dish is rather nice served with mashed potato.

1 227 g (8 oz) tin hot dog sausages (or ten sausages)
50 g (2 oz) butter
1 heaped dessertspoon cornflour
1 410 g (14½ oz) tin seedless grapes in syrup (you'll only need half the amount of grapes but all the syrup)
3 dessertspoons white wine
salt and freshly milled black pepper to taste

Gently fry the drained and dried sausages in the hot butter in a medium-sized saucepan for 2–3 minutes – then lift them out with a slotted spoon and set aside while you prepare the sauce. Using a small bowl thoroughly blend the cornflour in a little of the grape juice, then gradually incorporate it in the hot butter already in the pan. Slowly add the rest of the grape juice and half the tin of grapes, stirring all the time. When the sauce is thick add the white wine (if the sauce is not thick enough you may need a little more flour – it will depend on the amount of syrup found in the chosen brand of tinned grapes). Now put the sausages back in the pan, and season with salt and pepper. Spoon the sauce over the sausages and cook for 8–10 minutes.

Sausages in turmeric rice

Serves 3 Time taken: 15 minutes

120 ml (4 fl oz) water
½ teaspoon salt
1 small onion, finely sliced
large knob of butter
1½ teaspoons ground turmeric
1 260 g (9¼ oz) tin Uncle Ben's 'heat'n' serve' rice
1½ tablespoons sultanas (optional)
1 115 g (4 oz) tin cocktail sausages (or about 15 small sausages)
few sprigs of parsley to garnish

Add the salt to the water and boil in a medium-sized saucepan. While the water is boiling fry the onion slices in the hot butter in a separate pan until they begin turning brown, then blend in the turmeric. Now add the rice to the boiling water, followed by the onion and turmeric mixture and stir well until the ingredients are well blended. Add the sultanas, the drained sausages and mix well. Cook for 2–3 minutes until the sausages are hot and the rice cooked. Arrange on a serving dish and garnish with sprigs of parsley. Serve with a crisp lettuce.

Mashed potato boats with baked beans and sausages

Serves 4 | Time taken: 30 minutes

This is an ideal recipe for a children's party but if you wish to serve it on more formal occasions push the mash through a forcing bag to get a pretty shape.

1 154 g (5½ oz) packet instant mashed potato
knob of butter
50 g (2 oz) grated cheese (optional)
salt and freshly milled pepper
1 220 g (7¾ oz) tin baked beans in tomato sauce
1 115 g (4 oz) tin frankfurters (or 6 frankfurters)

Make the mashed potato according to the instructions on the packet. When this has been done and the potato is still hot, stir in a generous knob of butter as well as the grated cheese, the salt, and plenty of freshly milled pepper. These additions will greatly improve the taste and look of the mash.

Switch the oven on to 200°C, 400°F or Gas No. 6.

Butter a baking tray and spoon out the mashed potato on to it, dividing it into six portions. Then, with the back of a spoon hollow out centres, and pinch sides with your fingers to get a boat shape. Place beans inside them, top with the frankfurters, and bake for 15–20 minutes.

Dried haricot beans with sausages

Serves 3 | Prepare in advance (see below for details)

Like almost all dried vegetables, haricot beans need to soak overnight, so you will have to think in advance if you wish to make this dish. The beans will also need to be cooked in boiling water for 1½–2 hours. Cooking time, however, can be reduced considerably if you own a pressure cooker – the beans will then only take 20 minutes. If you do not possess one, put a pinch of bicarbonate of soda in the water when cooking the beans – they'll soften quicker that way.

227 g (8 oz) dried haricot beans
1 115 g (4 oz) tin party sausages (or about 15 very small sausages)
4 tablespoons oil
1 small onion, finely sliced
150 ml (¼ pint) white wine
juice of 1½ lemons

Soak the beans overnight in plenty of water. When ready, cover with water and cook on a high heat at first then simmer gently. Cook until the beans are soft and drain well.

Fry the sausages in 2–3 tablespoons of the oil for a few minutes then take them out with a slotted spoon. Fry the sliced onion in the same oil until lightly brown, then add the beans and stir for two minutes or so. Pour the wine in and cook on a high heat until it reduces. Add the rest of the oil, the lemon juice, the sausages and simmer for 5–10 minutes. Serve immediately with crispy French bread.

Sausage and artichoke salad in lemony vinaigrette

Serves 3–4 — Time taken: 15 minutes

This salad is ideal if you're entertaining a couple of friends for a snack lunch on a summer's day. Serve with fresh bread.

4 large crispy lettuce leaves
1 227 g (8 oz) tin hot dog sausages in brine
1 400 g (14 oz) tin artichoke hearts, drained
3 large tomatoes
salt and freshly milled black pepper

For the dressing:
juice of 1 large lemon
4 tablespoons oil
1 dessertspoon mayonnaise
salt and freshly milled black pepper to taste

Wash the lettuce leaves first and let them dry off a little while you get the rest of the ingredients together. Drain the sausages well then slice them into 1 cm (½ in) pieces diagonally (they look much nicer cut that way). Put them in a salad bowl. Then cut the artichoke hearts and the tomatoes into quarters so that they are nice and chunky. If the tomatoes are very large you may need to cut them into more pieces. Add them to the bowl followed by the lettuce – just tear the leaves into small irregular pieces. Sprinkle salt and pepper on the salad then make the dressing by mixing all the ingredients together in the order given and pour over the salad. Toss well.

Mash, bangers and ratatouille

Serves 4–5 — Time taken: 15–20 minutes

Tinned ratatouille is very tasty and mixes well with mashed potato. You don't have to use sausages if you don't want to, but if you do, this dish will provide you with an 'all in' meal. Accompany with a salad.

1 154 g (5½ oz) packet mashed potato
generous knob of butter
1 227 g (8 oz) tin hot dog sausages in brine
1 400 g (14 oz) tin ratatouille

Set the oven to 200°C, 400°F Gas No. 6.
Use a deep ovenproof dish to make the mash as it will go straight into the oven once it's ready. Make the mashed potato using half milk/water instead of just water as directed: the addition of milk really does improve it. While it's still hot stir in the butter. Drain the sausages and place them over the mash followed by the ratatouille. Bake in the oven for 10–15 minutes.

Chicken

Chicken with peaches and wine

Serves 3 Time taken: 20 minutes

The combination of wine and peaches gives this recipe a very delicate and sweet flavour. It also looks very appetizing.

1 1445 g (3 lb 3 oz) tin whole cooked chicken
For the sauce:
1 411 g (14½ oz) sliced peaches
150 ml (¼ pint) red wine
1 teaspoon coriander seeds, crushed
knob of butter
1 small onion, very finely chopped
1½ tablespoons flour
salt and freshly milled black pepper

Read the instructions on the tin of chicken before taking the chicken out of the tin. Then do so very gently as the flesh is tender and apt to come away if the chicken is not handled carefully. Keep the stock in a bowl as you will need some of it for the sauce. The rest could be used to make chicken soup and could be served as a first course with this recipe to follow. (See 'Chicken Soup with Corn and Green Pepper' on p. 29.)

Place the chicken in a roasting tin, season with salt and pepper and roast for 10–15 minutes in an oven marked 180°C, 350°F or Gas No. 4 (or follow the instructions on the label).

Open the tin of peaches and put 5 dessertspoons of the juice into a mixing bowl. Add 5 tablespoons of the chicken stock, the wine, and the coriander seeds. Set aside while you make the roux.

In a saucepan heat the butter and fry the onion until soft. Gradually incorporate the flour and continue stirring while you gradually pour in the prepared wine mixture. When the sauce has thickened add the peaches and season according to taste. Do not sprinkle too much salt or pepper on as the sauce should remain sweet. Simmer for 5 minutes but no more otherwise the wine will be reduced too much. Pour over the hot chicken, spooning the liquid over it a few times and arrange the peaches round the chicken.

Chicken with onion and celery

Serves 4

Time taken: 15 minutes

large knob of butter
1 large onion, sliced
3 celery sticks, sliced
salt and freshly milled black pepper
½ teaspoon dried oregano
1 212 g (7½ oz) tin small grilling mushrooms in brine
1 397 g (14 oz) tin chicken in mushroom sauce

Heat the butter and fry the onion in a medium-sized saucepan. When the onion slices begin to get golden brown, put in the celery and fry for a few minutes. Add the salt, pepper, oregano and two tablespoons of the brine from the tin of mushrooms. Now stir gently and cook for 5–7 minutes with the lid on. Then add the chicken pieces, as well as the mushrooms (well drained of the brine) and mix all the ingredients very carefully together. Cook for 5 minutes and serve with rice or potatoes.

Sliced chicken in mushroom sauce

Serves 4 Time taken: 30 minutes

For the sauce:
knob of butter
1 onion, finely sliced
1 clove garlic, crushed
1 heaped tablespoon flour
For the stock: ¼ chicken cube dissolved in 150 ml (¼ pint) boiling water
150 ml (¼ pint) white wine
salt and freshly milled pepper
1 212 g (7½ oz) tin grilling mushrooms
1 340 g (12 oz) tin chicken breasts in jelly

Melt the butter in a saucepan and gently fry the onion and the garlic. Add the flour a little at a time while pouring in the hot stock, stirring constantly so that the stock thickens and stays smooth and without lumps. Pour in the wine, continue stirring and season. Drain all the water from the mushrooms and add them to the other ingredients in the saucepan and simmer for 5 minutes.

Turn on the oven to 180°C, 350°F or Gas No. 4.

Open the tin of chicken and cut it into six even slices and arrange in an ovenproof dish. Pour the sauce over it and bake for 15–20 minutes.

Pastry with savoury chicken filling

Serves 4–6 Time taken: 30 minutes

Although it sounds a little fiddly, this recipe is actually easy to make and it also looks attractive. It makes a nice change as an alternative to rice or potato if served with a roast, or you can simply serve it with additional hot vegetables or a mixed salad.

1 418 g (14¾ oz) tin chunky chicken in savoury white sauce
1 medium-sized onion, finely chopped
2 garlic cloves, finely chopped
1 tablespoon parsley, finely chopped
¼ teaspoon dried oregano
cayenne pepper and salt
1 454 g (1 lb) packet puff pastry

Put the contents of the chicken tin into a small saucepan and add the onion, garlic, parsley and oregano, and season with cayenne pepper and salt. Mix well with a wooden spoon until the mixture is fairly smooth. Cook for 3–4 minutes on a medium heat stirring continuously, then remove from the heat and put aside.

Before starting to prepare the pastry, preheat the oven to 200°C, 400°F or Gas No. 6.

Sprinkle the surface of your table or counter with flour before opening the packet of pastry, then roll out the dough with the help of a rolling pin. You can then give it whatever shape you like: either one big circle or crescent or cut it (with the help of a pastry cutter or even a glass) into various shapes to make individual portions. When you have done this, spread the filling evenly in the pastry case and roll it up. Press the sides and the ends well together to seal in the filling. Prick the pastry with a fork – this allows the air to escape and prevents the pastry from bursting and it also makes a pretty pattern. Line a baking tray with greaseproof paper and place the pie on it. Bake for 15–20 minutes.

Cannelloni stuffed with chicken

Serves 4–6

Preparation time: 15 minutes
Baking time: 25 minutes

A packet of cannelloni and just a few readily available tins is all that is needed for this quickly made and highly attractive dish.

1 418 g (14¾ oz) tin chunky chicken pieces in savoury white sauce
12 cannelloni
For garlic sauce:
2–3 tablespoons olive oil
2–3 garlic cloves, finely chopped
1 140 g (5 oz) tin tomato purée
200 ml (⅓ pint) water
1 teaspoon dry marjoram
salt and freshly milled black pepper

Preheat the oven to 220°C, 425°F or Gas No. 7.
Empty the contents of the tin of chicken into a small bowl, mix and break the lumps of chicken so that they are small enough to fit easily into the cannelloni. With a small spoon fill the cannelloni and arrange in a shallow, ovenproof dish. Make sure you fill the cannelloni properly, using up all the chicken.

Now make the sauce. In a small saucepan heat the oil and the garlic gently. Add the tomato purée and gradually pour in the water, stirring all the time. Add the marjoram. Season well with salt and plenty of black pepper, mix thoroughly and let the sauce come to the boil. Take off heat and pour over the cannelloni. Put into the hot oven for 20–25 minutes. Serve hot.

Chicken with prunes and brandy

Serves 4 Time taken: 15 minutes

For this delicious brandy-flavoured chicken recipe you must have tinned chicken pieces of reasonable size.

115 g (4 oz) mushrooms
large knob of butter
425 g (15 oz) tin prunes
1–2 tablespoons brandy
salt and freshly milled black pepper
397 g (14 oz) tin chicken in mushroom sauce

Wash, dry and cut the mushrooms into quarters. Put to one side. Drain the prunes through a sieve into a bowl.

In a medium-sized saucepan melt the butter, put in the mushrooms and briskly fry for a few minutes. Reduce the heat and add the prunes, brandy and season with salt and pepper. Mix gently, cooking for about two minutes.

Place the chicken pieces and gravy from the tin on top of the prunes and cook for 2–3 minutes until the gravy has blended with the ingredients. Spoon the gravy over the chicken pieces a few times. Then cover with a tight lid and cook for five minutes on a low heat.

Fish

Salmon with parsley sauce

Serves 4 Time taken: 15 minutes

2 212 g (7½ oz) tins pink salmon
1 15 g (½ oz) packet parsley sauce mix combined with 300 ml (½ pint) milk
3 teaspoons capers
3 tablespoons parsley and thyme stuffing mix

Set the oven to 200°C, 400°F or Gas No. 6.
Coarsely flake the salmon with a fork and place in a buttered ovenproof dish. Make the sauce according to the instructions on the packet, adding the capers when it has come to the boil. Sprinkle the parsley and thyme mix over the salmon, and pour the sauce on top. Sprinkle with a little more parsley and thyme and bake for 10–15 minutes.

Salmon and asparagus quiche

Serves 5–6 Time taken: 25–30 minutes

For this unusual and delectable quiche you will need 225 g (8 oz shortcrust pastry mix. Since this is not currently available in this quantity you will have to buy a larger amount than is required. (See 'Peach Tart' on p. 121 for storage hints.) You will also need a 20 cm (8 in) round cake tin.

225 g (8 oz) shortcrust pastry mix
For the filling:
1 280 g (10 oz) tin asparagus tips
1 25 g (1 oz) packet cheese sauce mix combined with 300 ml (½ pint) milk
1 215 g (7½ oz) tin pink salmon
1 tablespoon double cream
salt and freshly milled pepper
a little Parmesan cheese

Read the instructions on the packet of mix and set the oven at the required temperature. Grease the bottom and part of the side of the tin. Mix the pastry with the recommended amount of water (we used 2 tablespoons) and press into a ball with your fingers. Now roll the dough out on a floured surface with a rolling pin and line the base of the tin with it as well as part of the side – to about 13 mm (½ in) high. Prick the pastry with a fork and bake for 15 minutes.

Drain the asparagus. Set 8 tips aside for decoration later and cut away the hard and stringy bottom part of the rest. Next make the filling by adding the milk to the cheese sauce mix or proceed as directed on the packet. When the sauce has boiled and thickened add the drained and flaked salmon followed by the asparagus tips. Mix gently, add the cream followed by the pepper to taste and simmer for 2–3 minutes. Pour the mixture into the prepared pastry case, sprinkle with a little pepper and some Parmesan cheese and decorate the top with the reserved asparagus. Bake for 5–10 minutes and serve the quiche with a salad. It is also very good cold.

Creamy salmon in puff pastry

Serves 5–6

Preparation time: 15 minutes
Baking time: 20 minutes

1 212 g (7½ oz) tin salmon
large knob of butter
1 tablespoon flour
250 ml (8½ fl oz) milk
2 tablespoons Parmesan cheese
salt and freshly milled pepper
pinch of nutmeg
1 454 g (1 lb) packet puff pastry

Drain the salmon well then make the sauce. Melt the butter in a saucepan and carefully incorporate the flour. Stir all the time while you gradually add the milk. When the sauce has thickened – it should be very thick and free of lumps – stir in the Parmesan cheese and season with the salt and pepper and the nutmeg. Draw off the heat and fold the flaked salmon into the creamy sauce.

Before starting to prepare the pastry, preheat the oven to 200°C, 400°F or Gas No. 6.

Now lightly flour your working surface and roll out the pastry with a rolling pin. The pastry for this recipe should not be rolled out too thinly. Spread the salmon mixture evenly over the pastry and roll it up. Press the ends and the sides well together to seal the case. Grease a baking tray with a little oil and place the roll on it. Prick holes all over it with a fork and bake in the oven for 20 minutes or until crisp and brown.

Serve with a salad.

Red salmon fish cakes

Serves 4

Time taken: 20 minutes

1 210 g (7½ oz) tin red salmon
large knob of butter
1 medium-sized onion, finely chopped
1 heaped tablespoon chopped parsley
25 g (1 oz) Parmesan cheese, grated
freshly milled black pepper
1 egg yolk
25 g (1 oz) flour
2–3 tablespoons milk
75 g (3 oz) breadcrumbs
oil for frying

Thoroughly drain the salmon, put it into a mixing bowl and mash up with a fork. Lightly beat the egg and put it in the bowl together with the onion, parsley, Parmesan cheese and black pepper.

In a medium-sized saucepan melt the butter, blend in the flour with a wooden spoon and stir over a low heat for 1 minute to make a roux. Gradually add the milk, stirring vigorously to avoid lumps.

Bring to the boil and simmer for 2–3 minutes. Remove the pan from the heat adding the salmon mixture from the bowl and mix well. Return to the heat and cook for 5 minutes stirring all the time.

Finally put the breadcrumbs on a plate and drop the mixture on to it a spoonful at a time. This will have to be done carefully as the mixture is rather soft at this stage. Then using both hands pat the crumbs evenly and firmly on both sides of the fish mixture. This should be done until all the mixture has been used and about 8 fish cakes obtained.

Heat the oil in a frying pan and fry the fishcakes on both sides for four minutes or until crisp and golden. Drain them on absorbent paper before serving.

Mackerel in white wine sauce

Serves 2–3

Time taken: 20 minutes

1 376 g (13¼ oz) tin white wine with cream sauce (sometimes called Cook-in Sauce)
1 198 g (7 oz) tin mackerel
1 425 g (15 oz) tin garden peas and small young carrots
a little ground nutmeg
salt and freshly milled black pepper to taste

Set your oven to 200°C, 400°F or Gas No. 6.
Cook the white wine sauce and bring to the boil on a low heat. Drain the mackerel well and if the pieces are large cut them in half sideways. Arrange them in a buttered ovenproof dish and pour the hot sauce over the mackerel. Then drain the tin of peas and carrots and if the carrots are large, split them down the middle. Mix about half the amount into the fish and wine (you can serve the rest of the peas and carrots separately) and sprinkle with a little nutmeg. Season with salt and pepper to taste. Bake for ten minutes or until hot and serve with mashed potato.

Herring fisherman's pie

Serves 4–5

Time taken: 20–25 minutes

1 200 g (7 oz) tin herrings in natural juice
1 17 g (½ oz) packet savoury white sauce mix combined with 300 ml (½ pint) milk
50 g (2 oz) split almonds
1 154 g (5½ oz) instant mashed potato
few knobs of butter
freshly milled pepper
a little grated Parmesan cheese

Set the oven to 200°C, 400°F or Gas No. 6.

Drain all the juice from the herrings and mash them with a fork. Make the savoury sauce as directed and when it has come to the boil stir in the fish followed by the almonds. Simmer for a minute or so then make the mashed potato. Follow the instructions on the packet but use half water and half milk instead of just water. The addition of milk will greatly improve the flavour of the mash. Place the fish mixture in a buttered ovenproof dish then evenly spread the mashed potato over it. Dot with butter, and sprinkle a little pepper and Parmesan cheese over the top. Bake for 10–15 minutes or until the pie is hot. You can also slip the pie under the grill for the last few minutes to brown the mashed potato.

Herrings with green olives and mustard sauce

Serves 4

Time taken: 15 minutes

1 190 g (6½ oz) tin herring fillets in paprika sauce
a few green olives (5–10)

For the sauce:
1 170 g (6 oz) tin Nestle's cream
1 heaped teaspoon mustard

Take the herrings out of the tin, place them in a bowl and break them up into small pieces with a fork. Keep the paprika sauce in the tin for the time being.

Open the tin of cream and thoroughly drain off all the excess water. Beat the cream in an electric mixer until creamy and light, add the mustard and pour the paprika sauce in. Beat for another few seconds.

Now, finely slice the olives and place them over the herrings. Pour the sauce over the fish and prick with a fork to allow cream to penetrate the mixture.

Scotch herrings and tomatoes gratinés

Serves 4

Time taken: 25–30 minutes

Tinned herrings and sardines are widely available in the shops. They are very useful for everyday cooking or for entertaining, and it is therefore surprising that they are not used more widely. There are many variations for really good *hors d'oeuvres* or main course dishes.

400 g (14 oz) tin of Scotch herrings in natural juice
6 medium-sized tomatoes
2 garlic cloves, finely chopped
1 heaped tablespoon parsley, finely chopped
4 tablespoons oil
salt and freshly ground black pepper
3 tablespoons dried breadcrumbs
2 heaped tablespoons grated cheese

Arrange the herrings in a shallow ovenproof dish after draining off all the excess liquid.

Put the tomatoes into a small bowl and cover with boiling water for 1–2 minutes until the skins split. Take the tomatoes out and peel them, then cut them into rough slices and drain off the excess liquid and seeds.

Preheat oven to 190°C, 375°F or Gas No. 5.

Now combine the tomatoes, garlic, parsley and oil in a small saucepan. Season with salt and plenty of pepper, mix gently and cook over a low heat for 3–5 minutes, depending on how well cooked you want them. Mix the sauce occasionally with a wooden spoon. When ready pour the mixture over the herrings, mix the breadcrumbs and cheese together and sprinkle over the dish. Bake in a hot oven for ten minutes and serve with additional vegetables.

Herring piquant

Serves 4

Time taken: 15 minutes

1 190 g (6½ oz) tin herring fillets in paprika sauce
1 medium green cooking apple
1 medium onion, finely chopped
2 hard-boiled eggs
1 teaspoon wine vinegar
salt and freshly milled black pepper
pinch of mace

Drain off a tablespoon of sauce from the tin, as there will be too much, and empty the remaining contents of the tin into a mixing bowl. Peel the apple, take the core out and grate into a bowl, and add the onion. With a fork, mash the eggs on a separate plate and add to the mixture in the bowl. Season with the vinegar, plenty of salt and pepper and mace to taste. Mix thoroughly while mashing the herring at the same time. Arrange in a long dish, pressing it down in patterns with a fork. Garnish with thinly sliced cucumber, apple or tomato.

Sardine and mushroom bake

Serves 4–5

Time taken: 20 minutes

If you would like a stronger taste of fish in this dish use 2 tins of sardines instead of one.

1 155 g (5½ oz) packet mashed potato
generous knob of butter
1 125 g (4½ oz) tin sardines in edible oil
1 20 g (¾ oz) packet mushroom white sauce mix combined with 300 ml (½ pint) milk
1 212 g (7½ oz) tin button mushrooms

Switch the oven to 200°C, 400°F or Gas No. 6.

Make the mashed potato according to the instructions on the packet but for the liquid use half water and half milk instead of just water: the addition of milk makes the mash fluffier. When the potato is ready and still hot add a knob of butter and mix well. Mash the sardines with the oil, using a fork, and add to the mashed potato stirring well until fully incorporated. Place the mixture in an ovenproof dish. Now make the sauce as directed on the packet and when this is ready add the drained mushrooms. Pour the mushroom sauce over the potato mixture and bake in the oven for 10–15 minutes or until hot.

Sardine snack

Serves 2 — Time taken: 20 minutes

An ideal snack for the unexpected guest who drops in for a chat.

2 slices brown bread
40 g (1½ oz) butter
1 heaped tablespoon flour
300 ml (½ pint) milk
1 small onion, finely chopped
1 teaspoon dried tarragon
1 tablespoon lemon juice
salt and freshly milled black pepper
1 egg yolk
1 tablespoon cream
125 g (4¼ oz) tin sardines in oil (there are usually four sardines in a tin)

Have ready the slices of fresh brown bread – home made or granary bread will taste best, but if only ordinary sliced bread is available, fry it in a little fat.

Melt two thirds of the butter in a saucepan, adding flour to make a roux. Gradually blend in the milk, stirring continuously over a low heat until this sauce is thick and smooth. Bring to the boil and cook for two minutes. Take off the heat.

Melt the remaining butter in a small frying pan and fry the onion until soft; then reduce the heat and put in the tarragon, lemon juice and season with salt and pepper. Stir and cook for one minute. When this is done add it to the sauce in the saucepan.

Now, in a separate bowl, lightly beat the egg yolk with the cream and add it to the sauce. Cook on a medium heat for three or four minutes taking care that it does not boil. Stir briskly whilst cooking.

Set out the sardines on the bread (two to each slice) and pour the sauce over. Serve hot.

Sardines in cream sauce

Serves 6

Preparation time: 15 minutes
Baking time: 15–20 minutes

4 120 g (4¼ oz) sardines in oil
1 212 g (7½ oz) tin grilling mushrooms
spring onions, finely sliced (about 6 shoots)
salt and freshly milled black pepper
lemon juice to taste
2 tablespoons butter
2 tablespoons flour
150 ml (¼ pint) milk
150 ml (¼ pint) single cream
3 tablespoons grated cheese
2 tablespoons breadcrumbs

Preheat oven to hot (200°C, 400°F or Gas No. 6).
Drain the sardines of the excess oil, break them up and put in a suitable shallow dish. Next, drain the mushrooms thoroughly, cut into quarters, and put in the dish. Add half the onions, season with salt and pepper and lemon to taste, mix and put aside.

Melt the butter in a small saucepan, add the flour, stir and cook for a minute. Gradually pour in the milk stirring all the time to avoid lumps, then add the cream. Season and cook for 2 minutes. Pour this sauce over the sardines and mix very gently.

Mix the grated cheese with the breadcrumbs and toss over the sauce. Sprinkle with the remaining onions and bake in the oven for 15–20 minutes or until golden brown. Serve immediately.

Grilled pilchards flavoured with lemon and parsley

Serves 2–3

Time taken: 15 minutes

If you wish to make this simple recipe for more people, just buy an extra tin of pilchards and be a little sparing with the 'coat-and-cook' mix – if you are, there should be just enough to coat another 5 or 6 pilchards.

1 454 g (1 lb) tin pilchards
1 70 g (2½ oz) packet 'coat-and-cook mix'
lemon slices and sprigs of parsley to garnish

Switch on your grill to a high temperature.
Thoroughly drain the pilchards and dry them on absorbent paper. Dip them into the mix, so that they are well covered on both sides and place them in a well-greased shallow oven dish or baking tray. Grill for 5–10 minutes (see instructions on the packet) and serve straight away garnished with slices of lemon and sprigs of parsley.

Pilchards Catalan

Serves 4–6

Time taken: 30 minutes

1 454 g (1 lb) tin pilchards in brine
knob of butter
2 medium-sized Spanish onions, coarsely sliced
3 garlic cloves, crushed
1 70 g (2½ oz) tin tomato purée
1 397 g (14 oz) tin tomatoes
½ teaspoon dried crushed chillies (from a jar or packet)

Separate the pilchards from the brine and arrange them in a shallow ovenproof dish.

Preheat oven to 200°C, 425°F or Gas No. 7.

Melt the butter in a saucepan and fry the onions until golden brown. Add the garlic and fry for a few seconds. Stir in the tomato purée then the tomatoes and the chillies. Mix gently but thoroughly and cook for 2 minutes. Pour the mixture over the pilchards and bake in the oven for 25 minutes.

Tuna à la royale

Serves 4

Time taken: 15 minutes

50 g (2 oz) butter
50 g (2 oz) fresh mushrooms, thinly chopped
1 heaped tablespoon flour
1 chicken cube dissolved in 150 ml (¼ pint) boiling water
salt and freshly milled black pepper
150 ml (¼ pint) single cream
1 198 g (7 oz) tin tuna fish
1 heaped tablespoon parsley, finely chopped

Melt the butter in a saucepan and gently fry the mushrooms. When they are ready take them out and put to one side. Add the flour to the butter remaining in the saucepan, doing it gradually to avoid lumps. Now slowly add the chicken stock making sure that a smooth and even texture is obtained every time more liquid is introduced. Add the seasoning and cream and cook for 2 minutes. Take the saucepan off the heat.

Now drain the tin of tuna of excess oil, break it up with a fork and add it to the sauce together with the mushrooms and parsley. Mix gently but thoroughly. Cook for another 2 minutes.

Serve hot with plain boiled rice or garlic bread.

Macaroni cheese and tuna bake

Serves 3–4 | Time taken: 20 minutes

The combination of macaroni and tuna with cheese topping really is good and should prove popular, especially with children.

- 1 425 g (15 oz) tin macaroni cheese
- 1 198 g (7 oz) tuna fish
- 1 25 g (1 oz) cheese sauce mix combined with 300 ml (½ pint) milk
- freshly milled black pepper

Set the oven to 200°C, 400°F or Gas No. 6.

Place the macaroni cheese in an ovenproof dish and add the flaked tuna fish. Make the cheese sauce according to the instructions on the packet and pour it over the macaroni and tuna. Sprinkle with pepper and bake in the hot oven for 10–15 minutes.

Serve with another vegetable as the sauce is quite rich.

Tuna with mushrooms and paprika

Serves 3 | Time taken: 20 minutes

- 50 g (2 oz) butter
- 112 g (4 oz) medium-sized mushrooms, finely sliced (stalks as well)
- 2 garlic cloves, finely sliced
- 1 tablespoon flour
- *For the stock*: 1 chicken cube dissolved in 300 ml (½ pint) boiling water
- 1 heaped tablespoon parsley, chopped
- 3 pieces red pickled paprika (or pickled red peppers) from a jar and cut into thin strips
- 1 198 g (7 oz) tin tuna fish
- salt and freshly milled black pepper
- 2 tablespoons double cream

Begin by melting the butter in a medium-sized saucepan, then fry the mushrooms and garlic in it for a few minutes. When softened, remove the mushrooms from the pan and put them on a plate, leaving the butter in the saucepan. Gradually incorporate the flour into the butter as well as a little of the stock. Stir the mixture well until smooth and creamy, add the remaining stock and cook for 2–3 minutes on a low heat. Now stir in the parsley and paprika as well as the fried mushrooms and garlic. Break up the tuna fish with a fork into fairly large pieces, add to the other ingredients and season, putting the emphasis on the pepper rather than the salt. Mix well and cook for another 1–2 minutes, then remove the pan from the heat and stir in the cream. Serve hot and with plain boiled rice.

Cannelloni filled with prawn and mushroom sauce

Serves 3–4 Time taken: 35 minutes

This recipe is for a small number of people unless you want to use more than one tin of prawns. In that case simply multiply the other ingredients by the number of tins you use.

1 198 g (7 oz) prawns in brine
1 heaped tablespoon parsley, finely chopped
1 tablespoon olive oil
1 garlic clove, crushed
8 cannelloni tubes from a 250 g (8¾ oz) packet

For the sauce:
50 g (2 oz) butter
2 tablespoons flour

For the stock: ½ chicken cube dissolved in 150 ml (¼ pint) of water
150 ml (¼ pint) milk
115 g (4 oz) fresh mushrooms, finely sliced (tinned mushrooms can be used)
salt and freshly milled black pepper
1–2 tablespoons sherry

Switch on oven to 220°C, 425°F or Gas No. 7.

Drain the prawns and rinse them in cold water. Mix with half the amount of parsley, the oil and garlic. Fill the cannelloni with this mixture and place in a shallow ovenproof dish. If you have difficulty in filling the cannelloni stand them upright on a saucer. When filled, cover the top with your finger and tip over, placing the cannelloni in the dish. Put aside the dish of cannelloni and start preparing the sauce.

In a small saucepan on a low heat melt the butter. Add the flour and mix vigorously to avoid lumps. Take off the heat and pour in the stock, a little at a time, stirring continuously and taking care to obtain a smooth blend every time some more liquid has been added. Return to the heat, continuing to stir whilst pouring in the milk gradually. As soon as the sauce comes to the boil put in the mushrooms, and the rest of the parsley. Season well with salt and pepper and pour in the sherry. Stir and cook for 2 minutes. When ready pour the mixture over the cannelloni and put in the hot oven for 20 minutes.

Odd-tin-out

Cannelloni filled with aubergines in tomato and garlic sauce

Serves 4–6

Time taken: 35 minutes

1 400 g (14 oz) tin aubergine slices
12 cannelloni from a 250 g ($8\frac{3}{4}$ oz) packet
For the sauce:
1–2 tablespoons olive oil
2–3 garlic cloves
$\frac{1}{2}$ of 142 g (5 oz) tin tomato purée
1 teaspoon dry marjoram
salt and freshly milled black pepper
200 ml ($\frac{1}{3}$ pint) water

Preheat oven to 220°C, 425°F or Gas No. 7.

Drain the excess oil from the aubergines and put it to one side to use for the sauce. Mash the aubergine slices a little so they will easily fit into the cannelloni. Now stuff the cannelloni with the mashed aubergine and put into an ovenproof dish. If there are any over they can be added to the sauce at the next stage to give flavour.

To make the sauce, heat the oil and fry the garlic gently in a small saucepan. Add the tomato purée, any leftover aubergine, the aubergine oil, the marjoram and the salt and pepper. Pour in the water very gradually, stirring continuously. Cook for 2 minutes. Take off the heat and pour over the cannelloni. Put the dish into the hot oven for 20 minutes.

Cannelloni filled with vegetables in tomato sauce

Serves 4–6

Time taken: 35 minutes

1 212 g (7½ oz) tin button mushrooms in brine
1 stick celery, very finely chopped
1 heaped tablespoon parsley, very finely chopped
1–2 garlic cloves crushed
½ teaspoon celery seed, crushed
salt and freshly milled black pepper
4 tablespoons olive oil
12 cannelloni out of a 250 g (8¾ oz) packet
1 298 g (10½ oz) tin mushroom and tomato sauce
3–4 tablespoons hot water

Preheat oven to 220°C, 425°F or Gas No. 7.
Put the mushrooms in a sieve, giving them a good shake to drain off the brine. Cut the mushrooms into quarters and put them into a mixing bowl. Add the celery, half the parsley and the garlic. Season with half the amount of celery seed and salt and pepper. Pour in half the olive oil and mix thoroughly. Fill the cannelloni with this mixture and arrange in a shallow, ovenproof dish.

Put the contents of the tin of mushroom and tomato sauce into a small mixing bowl, add the remaining parsley, celery seed and oil. Dilute with a little water because the sauce is quite thick; adjust the seasoning by adding more if required. Pour the sauce over the cannelloni. Put in the hot oven for 20–25 minutes.

Pasta shells in tomato sauce

Serves 4

Time taken: 20–25 minutes

275 g (10 oz) pasta shells
knobs of butter
salt
50–75 g (2–3 oz) grated cheese
For the sauce:
1½ tablespoons finely chopped onion
2–3 tablespoons oil
1 281 (10 oz) tin spaghetti sauce
¾ teaspoon dried herbs
142 ml (5 fl oz) single cream
salt and freshly milled black pepper

Begin by cooking the pasta following the instructions on the packet. While this is in hand, make the sauce by gently frying the onion in the hot oil for a minute or so. Then add the spaghetti sauce, followed by the herbs and stir well. Just before the pasta is ready pour the cream into the tomato sauce and season with salt and pepper. Now add a knob of butter and some salt to the drained pasta and put in an ovenproof dish. Pour the sauce over it and mix well. Sprinkle the cheese evenly on top and dot with butter. Brown under the grill and serve straight away.

Pasta in tomato sauce with mushrooms and meatballs

Serves 4 | Time taken: 20–25 minutes

This delicious and quickly made tomato sauce with meatballs and mushrooms is ideal to serve with pasta.

4–6 tablespoons oil
1 small onion, finely chopped
2 small garlic cloves, finely sliced
1 140 g (5 oz) tin tomato purée
300 ml (½ pint) boiling water
1 heaped teaspoon dried herbs
1 425 g (15 oz) tin meatballs in brown sauce
1 212 g (7½ oz) tin whole mushrooms
salt and freshly milled black pepper
pasta (tagliatelle if possible) for four
Parmesan cheese (optional)

Heat some of the oil in a medium-sized saucepan and fry the onion and garlic in it. Stir in the tomato purée, add the boiling water, the herbs and the rest of the oil and mix well. Simmer for a few minutes. Now thoroughly drain all the gravy from the meatballs as well as all the liquid from the tin of mushrooms and fry them in a little oil until brown. Place the meatballs and mushrooms in the tomato sauce and give all the ingredients a good stir. Season well and leave to simmer for 10–15 minutes until thick. If you have time cook for a little longer as it will improve the taste.

Cook the pasta the way you normally do – we normally sprinkle with salt and pepper and add a generous knob of butter after draining – and put in a nice serving dish. Pour the prepared sauce over the pasta or serve separately if preferred and with Parmesan cheese.

Tagliatelle and aubergines in white sauce

Serves 4 | Time taken: 25–30 minutes

227 g (8 oz) packet quick tagliatelle
knob of butter
salt and freshly milled pepper
1 368 g (13 oz) tin fried aubergine slices

For the sauce:
knob of butter
40 g (1½ oz) flour
600 ml (1 pint) milk
75 g (3 oz) grated cheese
salt and freshly milled pepper

Preheat the oven to 200°C, 400°F or Gas No. 6.

To cook the pasta follow the directions on the packet.

Meanwhile, make the sauce. Melt the knob of butter in a pan and gradually incorporate the flour, stirring all the time to prevent lumps from forming. Slowly add the milk and mix well until the flour has thoroughly blended into the milk. When the sauce is smooth and has thickened stir in 25 g (1 oz) of the cheese and season with salt and pepper.

Now drain the cooked tagliatelle well, add a knob of butter, and the salt and pepper. Arrange it in a large ovenproof dish (if it's too small the pasta will stick together) and mix the separated slices of aubergine into it. Then pour the sauce over the pasta and aubergines, mixing well with a spoon to allow the sauce to soak right through. Sprinkle with the rest of the cheese and dot with butter. Bake for 15 minutes.

Spinach quiche

Serves 6–8

Preparation time: 15 minutes
Baking time: 25 minutes

This is a rather versatile dish. It can be served either as a starter or as a main course and could be accompanied by a variety of salads.

1 454 g (1 lb) shortcrust pastry mix

For the filling:

1 736 g (1 lb 10 oz) tin spinach purée
25 g (1 oz) butter
juice of ½ lemon
3 eggs
300 ml (½ pint) double cream
2 tablespoons finely chopped onion
2 tablespoons Parmesan cheese
pinch of nutmeg
salt and freshly milled black pepper

Make the pastry according to the instructions on the packet. Grease a 25 cm (10 in) quiche tin, then line it with the pastry. Put it in a preheated oven (the temperature will be mentioned on the packet) and bake it for 10–15 minutes or until the pastry starts turning brown.

While the pastry is in the oven make the filling. Thoroughly drain the spinach in a sieve pressing with the back of a spoon to squeeze all the excess water out. Then put it in a pan together with the butter and the lemon and cook until hot. Stir to ensure that the butter has blended into the spinach. In a separate bowl, whip the eggs lightly with a fork and beat in the cream. Add the chopped onion, Parmesan cheese and nutmeg and mix thoroughly. Now incorporate this mixture into the spinach and season well (tinned spinach requires a lot of salt and pepper). The pastry should now be ready. Take it out of the oven and place on a baking tray before pouring the spinach mixture into the pastry case. Do not worry if the mixture appears to be a little runny, it will soon set in the oven. Bake for 25 minutes at 190°C, 375°F or Gas No. 5.

Savoury nut mix with spinach

Serves 4–6 Time taken: 30 minutes

These are tasty savoury cakes especially appreciated by the health food addict or vegetarian. And they are just as nourishing as meat or fish.

1 egg
227 g (8 oz) from a rissole nut meat packet (usually sold in 12 oz packets)
496 (18 oz) tin spinach leaf in salted water
freshly ground black pepper to taste
oil for frying

Mix the egg and the rissole meat in a mixing bowl. Drain a little water off the spinach into a cup, and keep as a reserve. Add the spinach to the mixing bowl, season well with pepper, and mix thoroughly – the mixture should be firm, not crumbly. If the mixture is a little dry add some of the reserved liquid to moisten it.

Take a little extra time with the mixing, making sure that all the ingredients are well blended. Mould the mixture into cakes and fry them in a little hot oil on a medium heat for 2–3 minutes each side or until golden brown.

Serve with mashed potatoes and plain steamed vegetables (carrots or cabbage) and with a piquant sauce or mango chutney.

Onion and potato omelette

Serves 3 Time taken: 15 minutes

For the omelette:
6 eggs
2 tablespoons milk
salt and freshly milled black pepper
large knob of butter

For the filling:
1 small onion, finely sliced
large knob butter
1 283 g (10 oz) tin new potatoes
50 g (2 oz) grated cheese
salt and freshly milled black pepper

In a mixing bowl thoroughly beat the eggs together with the milk, then add the salt and pepper. Set aside for a moment while you make the filling. Brown the sliced onion in the hot butter first, then the sliced potatoes. After a few minutes stir in the grated cheese, the pepper and the salt. Remove from the heat.

Melt the butter in a largish frying pan and when it's hot pour in the egg mixture. When this has nearly set (the outside should be firm but the inside still quite soft) place the potato mixture on one half of the omelette. Fold the other half of the omelette over it and cook for 2–3 minutes. Do not leave it on too long or else it will dry up – a good omelette should be soft inside. Serve immediately.

Mushroom omelette

Serves 2

Time taken: 10 minutes

For the filling:
1 212 g (7½ oz) tin button mushrooms in brine
knob of butter
1 tablespoon double cream
salt and freshly milled black pepper

For the omelette:
4 eggs
1½ tablespoons milk
salt and freshly milled black pepper
knob of butter

In a small pan toss the mushrooms in the hot butter for a minute or two, then add the cream followed by the salt and pepper. Stir with a wooden spoon until the cream has thickened a little.

Now beat the eggs and the milk thoroughly in a mixing bowl, add the salt and pepper and mix well. Heat the butter in an omelette pan and pour the egg mixture in. When the outside of the omelette has set but the inside is still soft, place the mushroom mixture on to one side of the omelette and fold the other side over. Cook for 2 minutes or so and serve straight away.

Spinach pancakes in white sauce

Serves 4–5

Preparation time: 25 minutes
Baking time: 20 minutes

1 283 g (10 oz) tin spinach purée
generous knob of butter
salt and freshly milled black pepper
1 125 g (4½ oz) packet lemon-flavoured pancake mix which will require the addition of 1 egg

For the sauce:
knob of butter
2½ tablespoons flour
600 ml (1 pint) milk
75 g (3 oz) grated cheese
pinch ground nutmeg
salt and freshly milled black pepper

Drain the spinach purée well and put in a saucepan together with the knob of butter, the salt and the pepper. Simmer on a low heat until hot. Make the pancakes according to the directions on the packet and pile them flat on a plate as you go along.

Now make the sauce by melting the butter in a saucepan, adding the flour a little at a time while incorporating the milk. Continue stirring until thick, then add three-quarters of the grated cheese, the nutmeg, salt and pepper. Stir 4 tablespoons of this sauce into the hot spinach.

Preheat the oven to 200°C, 400°F or Gas No. 6.

Now fill each pancake with some spinach mixture and place in an ovenproof dish. Carry on doing this until you've used up all the spinach. You should have enough mixture to fill about 10 pancakes if a 20 cm (8 in) frying pan is used. Pour the sauce over the pancakes, sprinkle with the remaining cheese and dot with butter. Bake for 20 minutes.

Salade Niçoise

Serves 4–6 Time taken: 15 minutes

This salad makes an excellent and popular start to a meal. It can also be served as a main course for lunch with French bread and butter and a glass of white wine. Serve it in individual dishes or as a large salad.

1 large lettuce heart
150 ml (¼ pint) pre-prepared salad dressing of oil, vinegar, salt and pepper
280 g (10 oz) tin red kidney beans, drained of liquid
1 large fresh green pepper
1 medium-sized onion, thinly sliced into rings
200 g (7 oz) tin tuna fish
115 g (4 oz) black olives
3–4 firm tomatoes
3 hard-boiled eggs
50 g (2 oz) tin anchovy fillets

Wash the lettuce leaves, drain well and get them as dry as possible. Tear the large lettuce leaves into pieces. Then pour half the amount of salad dressing into a large salad bowl followed by the lettuce and beans. Toss the salad well.

Next cut the green pepper in half, removing the seeds, and slice thinly. Add to the salad together with the onion rings.

Open the tin of tuna and drain off the excess oil. Break the tuna into small pieces and put into the salad bowl followed by the olives. Cut the tomatoes and the eggs into quarters and arrange the pieces around the bowl. Then pour the remaining salad dressing over the salad. Put on a platter and decorate by placing the anchovy fillets between the egg and tomatoes.

Accompaniments

The recipes in this section are ideal for serving with dishes from the Main Course section, with a roast of some kind or even with cold left-overs. Why not try a crunchy 'Walnuts and Artichoke Salad' with cold roast beef; delicious 'Corn Fritters' with roast chicken; 'Spinach *à la Crème*' with 'Beef Paprika' from the Main Course section; or a cool and spicy salad like 'Grapefruit and Cucumber' with cold tongue. These are only suggestions, of course, and there are many more combinations which readers will discover for themselves.

Pasta salad

Serves 4–6

Time taken: 15 minutes

50 g (2 oz) pasta shells or any other similar pasta
2–3 tablespoons thick mayonnaise
1 teaspoon French mustard
1 small onion, finely chopped
12–15 black olives, stoned and halved
1 198 g (7 oz) tin of ham

Simmer the pasta shells in a pan of boiling salted water for about 7 minutes or until tender. Drain well when cooked.

In a serving bowl mix the mayonnaise and mustard together, then add the onion and the olives. Open the tin of ham and remove all excess fat. Cut it into thin strips more or less the same size as the shells and add to the bowl. Now put the pasta in and stir all the ingredients thoroughly together.

Serve with a green salad.

Sweetcorn and pickled onion salad

Serves 4–5 Time taken: 10 minutes

This salad looks very decorative and the pickled onions give it a sharp flavour.

- 1 340 g (12 oz) tin sweetcorn with peppers
- 1 170 g (6 oz) jar white cocktail pickled onions
- 3 tablespoons French dressing
- 3 tablespoons mayonnaise
- 1 small fresh green pepper and chopped parsley to garnish

Thoroughly drain the sweetcorn and arrange in a dish. Add the drained pickled onions and mix well. In a separate bowl combine the French dressing and mayonnaise together and stir it into the salad. Wash the pepper, cut into strips, and arrange decoratively over the salad. Sprinkle with some parsley.

Walnut and artichoke salad

Serves 4–6 Time taken: 10 minutes

This is a really delicious salad. The contrast between soft artichoke, the crispy celery and crunchy nuts is very appetizing. The red paprika adds colour as well as taste. It is a particularly useful dish for parties because a large quantity of salad can be made quickly with little extra effort.

- 1 400 g (14 oz) tin artichoke hearts
- 2–3 sticks of celery, thinly sliced
- 2–3 sticks of red pickled paprika from a tin, sliced into thin strips
- 2 heaped tablespoons peanuts
- 2 heaped tablespoons walnuts, broken in halves

For the dressing:

- 4 tablespoons oil
- 1 tablespoon wine vinegar
- 1–2 garlic cloves, crushed
- salt and freshly milled black pepper

Thoroughly drain the water from the artichokes – it may be helpful to put the hearts with the flower side down to ensure the water thoroughly drains off. Then make the French dressing by combining all the ingredients and mixing thoroughly in a medium-sized bowl. Cut the artichokes into halves and put into the bowl. Now add the rest of the ingredients and mix carefully but thoroughly. Taste to make sure it is well seasoned.

Egg and beetroot salad

Serves 4 Time taken: 15 minutes

This is a perfect salad for a cold buffet.

1 teaspoon dry mustard
1 teaspoon castor sugar
salt and freshly milled black pepper
1 tablespoon wine vinegar
1 tablespoon horseradish
4 tablespoons thick mayonnaise
3 tablespoons double cream
3–4 spring onions, finely chopped
1 220 (7¾ oz) beetroot in salted water
1 227 g (8 oz) butter beans
4 hard-boiled eggs, halved

In a bowl mix the mustard, sugar, salt and pepper with the vinegar. Then add the horseradish, 1 tablespoon of the mayonnaise, 2 tablespoons of the cream and stir well. Now put in the chopped onions, the drained beetroot and butter beans and mix thoroughly. Transfer the mixture into the middle of a serving dish and arrange the egg halves round the edge. In a separate bowl mix the remaining mayonnaise and cream together and pour over the eggs.

Cold pimento rice salad

Serves 6–7 Time taken: 25 minutes

In this recipe we've given quantities for average helpings but this versatile salad can easily be adapted to serve a larger number of people. It's in fact a perfect party dish: tasty, decorative and economical.

227 g (8 oz) rice
For the tomato sauce:
half an onion, finely chopped
4–5 tablespoons oil
5 teaspoons tomato purée (from a tin or tube)
200 ml (⅓ pint) boiling water
salt and freshly milled black pepper

For the dressing:
2 dessertspoons oil
1½ dessertspoons vinegar
1½ dessertspoons tomato ketchup
1½ dessertspoons Worcestershire sauce
1 190 g (6¾ oz) tin whole sweet pimentos in brine

Cook the rice as you normally do or follow the instructions on the packet. Now make the tomato sauce: fry the chopped onion in the hot oil until lightly brown, add the condensed tomato purée followed by the boiling water, salt and pepper, finally give the sauce a good stir and cook with the lid off for 10–15 minutes.

Make the dressing by blending all the ingredients together in a bowl.

In a salad bowl, mix the cooled rice and the hot tomato sauce, add the dressing and thoroughly mix the salad. Drain the pimentos and cut each one into thin strips, add to the rice and mix well. Cool in the fridge before serving.

Butter bean salad

Serves 2–3 | Time taken: 10 minutes

This is a very decorative salad and can be made in larger quantities for buffet suppers. The butter beans make it substantial enough to serve on its own as a first course or as a main course dish with sardines or cold meats.

1 212 g (7½ oz) tin butter beans in salted water
2 sticks celery, finely chopped
1 small onion, finely chopped
1 heaped tablespoon parsley, finely chopped
3 tablespoons double cream
salt and freshly ground black pepper
2 tomatoes, thinly sliced
1 tablespoon grated cheese

Drain the water from the beans thoroughly and place them in a serving dish. Put the rest of the vegetables – except the tomatoes – in a separate bowl and pour in the cream, salt and pepper. Spoon this mixture over the butter beans. Lay the tomatoes over the vegetables and sprinkle the cheese on top.

Spicy kidney bean and mushroom salad

Serves 4 | Time taken: 10 minutes

This delicious salad, with its attractive smell and flavour can be served as an *hors d'oeuvre* with a slice of fresh brown country loaf and some butter, or with cold meats and sausages.

227 g (8 oz) fresh small mushrooms
1 large onion, finely chopped
2 garlic cloves, finely chopped
1 heaped tablespoon fresh parsley, finely chopped
¼ head fennel, finely sliced (use celery instead if fennel is not available)
3–4 small pickled onions, thinly sliced
1 430 g (15¼ oz) tin red kidney beans
4 tablespoons oil
1 tablespoon lemon juice
sprinkle of cayenne pepper and salt

Wash the mushrooms thoroughly, drain well and slice them (the stalks should be sliced too). Arrange in a serving bowl and add the onion, garlic, parsley and fennel as well as the pickled onions. Drain the beans and add them to the bowl. Now pour the oil and lemon juice in and season with cayenne pepper and salt. Mix well.

Anchovy, olive and mushroom salad

Serves 4–5 Time taken: 10 minutes

This strong-flavoured mix may be served alongside a grill or as a starter on its own or even with other salads and accompanied with fresh granary bread and butter.

50 g (2 oz) tin anchovy fillets
10–15 large green olives
212 g (7½ oz) tin button mushrooms in brine
1 medium-sized onion, very finely chopped
freshly milled black pepper
1 tablespoon double cream

Drain off excess oil from the anchovy fillets and slice them finely. Take the stones out of the olives and chop very finely. Strain the mushrooms, rinse them under cold water and cut them up very finely. In a serving dish combine all the chopped ingredients, add a little black pepper, the cream and mix thoroughly.

Mixed bean salad

Serves 7–8 Time taken: 10 minutes

Most varieties of tinned beans make nice salads. Though they sometimes lack flavour, they can be quickly brought to life with the addition of a few strong ingredients. Try this combination.

1 425 g (15 oz) tin broad beans
1 425 g (15 oz) kidney beans
1 425 g (15 oz) tin French beans
1 medium onion, very finely sliced
a little salt and freshly milled black pepper

For the dressing:
5 tablespoons oil
2½ tablespoons vinegar
1 dessertspoon mayonnaise
2 garlic cloves, crushed
1 level teaspoon dried mixed herbs
salt and freshly milled black pepper

Tip out all liquid from the tinned vegetables then swirl cold water over them and drain in a colander. Place all the beans in a salad bowl and mix in the onion. Sprinkle with salt and pepper. Now make the salad dressing by combining all the ingredients together in the order mentioned and pour over the vegetables. Let the salad stand for a few minutes before serving to allow the dressing to be soaked up.

Curried potato salad

Serves 4 | Time taken: 10 minutes

The tinned curry sauce used here makes this a highly flavoured recipe – good as a main dish or accompaniment. Made in larger amounts it is useful for parties.

2 540 g (1 lb 3 oz) tins potatoes
1 large pickled cucumber, finely chopped
3 spring onions, finely chopped
1 stick celery, finely sliced
2 hard-boiled eggs, quartered
1 tablespoon sultanas
1 370 g (13 oz) tin curry sauce

Put all the ingredients into a salad bowl, mix very gently but thoroughly, taking care not to break the eggs or the other ingredients. Additional salt and pepper should not be necessary but you may want to add more.

Serve with cold meat.

Grapefruit and cucumber salad

Serves 4–5 | Time taken: 15 minutes

This is a curry-flavoured fruit and vegetable salad. It can be served as an accompaniment to cold chicken or ham but is substantial enough to be eaten on its own or as an *hors d'oeuvre.*

For the dressing:
5 tablespoons olive oil
2–3 tablespoons wine vinegar
½ teaspoon hot chilli powder
½ teaspoon dry mustard
salt and freshly milled black pepper
½ teaspoon of sugar (optional)

1 540 g (1 lb 3 oz) tin grapefruit segments in natural juice and unsweetened
½ cucumber, sliced and peeled if preferred
3 spring onions, finely chopped
1 heaped tablespoon chopped walnuts
1 heaped tablespoon sultanas
1 large lettuce head

In a mixing bowl combine the oil, vinegar, chilli powder, mustard, salt and pepper – if you like a slightly sweetened flavour to your dressing add sugar. Stir the ingredients well.

Put the salad ingredients, leaving out the lettuce, into a bowl with the dressing. Mix well but gently so as not to break the grapefruit segments. Now make a bed of lettuce in a serving bowl and fill with the spicy salad.

Serve with granary bread and butter.

Beetroot in soured cream

Serves 4

Time taken: 7 minutes

1 142 g (5 fl oz) carton soured cream
3–4 spring onions, finely sliced
salt and freshly milled black pepper
¼ teaspoon ground mixed spice
2–3 pickled onions, finely sliced (optional)
1 220 g (7¾ oz) sliced beetroot in salted water

Put the soured cream into a serving bowl together with the onions, salt and pepper, the spice and the pickled onions if required. Mix thoroughly, then gently fold in the drained beetroot until it is well coated with soured cream.

Spinach à la crème

Serves 4

Time taken: 10 minutes

1 454 g (1 lb) tin spinach leaf
knob of butter
freshly milled black pepper
2 tablespoons double cream

Drain the spinach well in a colander, pressing down with a spoon to remove excess water. Then put the spinach in a saucepan with knob of butter and pepper to taste. Before it reaches the boil mix in the cream and stir gently.

Green peas – French style

Serves 3–4

Time taken: 15 minutes

Here is a recipe which will help enhance an ordinary tin of peas – an easy recipe to fall back on if you're in a hurry.

50 g (2 oz) butter
1 onion, finely sliced
3 large lettuce leaves
½ teaspoon sugar
1 283 g (10 oz) tin peas
1 teaspoon fresh parsley or mint, finely chopped
pinch of salt

Melt the butter in a saucepan and gently fry the onion until it begins to turn brown. Wash the lettuce leaves and pat dry with a towel. Cut them into thin strips and add to the pan. Cook for a few minutes or until they've become soft. Add the sugar, the peas and about 3–4 dessertspoons of the liquid in the tin, or just enough to almost cover them. Stir in the parsley or mint and the salt. Cook until hot or according to the instructions on the tin, but do not overcook or they'll become mushy.

Sweetcorn fritters

Serves 5 Time taken: 20 minutes

Corn fritters make a welcome change from potatoes or rice and go well with roasts or fish.

115 g (4 oz) flour
pinch of salt
1 egg
150 ml (¼ pint) milk
1 325 g (11½ oz) tin sweetcorn, drained
freshly milled black pepper
oil for frying

Sift the flour and the salt into a mixing bowl. Make a well in the centre, put in the egg and gradually stir in half the milk. Mix vigorously for a few minutes then add the rest of the milk and beat the mixture thoroughly until it is smooth and creamy. Now stir in the corn and season with pepper.

Heat some oil in a frying pan and drop large spoonfuls of the mixture in it. Fry as many spoonfuls as you have room for but leave enough space between each fritter as the mixture tends to spread. Brown on both sides then drain on absorbent paper. Serve straight away.

Spinach and potato curry

Serves 4–5 Time taken: 15 minutes

This is a dry and tasty curry which is quickly made and filling. It is a useful recipe to have at your fingertips to serve with meat or chicken.

50 g (2 oz) butter
1 medium onion, finely sliced
1 level teaspoon ground turmeric
1 level teaspoon chilli powder
1 teaspoon ground ginger
1 538 g (1 lb 3 oz) tin new potatoes
1 482 g (1 lb 1 oz) tin spinach leaf
salt to taste

Melt the butter in a saucepan and gently fry the onion. Before using the spices try a little in your hand, as the quantities will depend to a certain extent on their strength and your own taste. Stir in the turmeric, chilli powder and ginger and leave on a low heat while you get the potatoes ready. Drain these and cut the large ones into about 3 slices and the small ones in half. Add them to the pan and mix thoroughly so they get well coated with the spices. Stir in the drained spinach but do this rather carefully as tinned spinach is already quite soft and can easily look mushy. Add a sprinkle of salt and cook with the lid on for 5–10 minutes.

Sauerkraut with apple sauce

Serves 4–6

Time taken: 12 minutes

454 g (16 oz) jar sauerkraut
50 g (2 oz) butter
425 g (15 oz) tin apple sauce
2 heaped tablespoons finely chopped dried apricots or 2 tablespoons sultanas
1–2 tablespoons lemon juice (optional)
pinch of cayenne pepper

Put the sauerkraut into a strainer and press with a wooden spoon to make sure all the liquid is drained off.

Melt the butter in a saucepan, put in the sauerkraut, apple sauce and apricots (or sultanas). Add the lemon juice and a pinch of cayenne pepper. Mix thoroughly, cover with a tight lid and cook for 5–10 minutes.

Serve hot with poultry, veal or pork.

Potatoes and stringless beans with sour cream

Serves 4–6

Time taken: 25 minutes

This is an appetizing all-vegetable recipe which is ideal for vegetarians. It also goes very well with fish.

490 g (17½ oz) tin new potatoes
397 g (14 oz) tin whole stringless beans in salted water
50 g (2 oz) butter
1 heaped tablespoon grated cheese
142 ml (5 fl oz) carton soured cream
1 heaped tablespoon parsley, finely chopped
salt and freshly milled black pepper

Preheat the oven to 200°C, 400°F or Gas No. 6.

Open the tins. Put the potatoes in a strainer, rinse under a cold tap and drain well. Then drain the beans. Next, arrange both the beans and potatoes in layers in a shallow, buttered ovenproof dish. Dot the top with butter and half the grated cheese. Mix the soured cream, half the parsley, salt and plenty of pepper in a small bowl. Stir well and pour over the vegetables. The remaining cheese should now be sprinkled over the top. Bake for 15 minutes, or until brown, in the hot oven.

Before serving garnish with the remaining parsley.

Carrots in rich béchamel sauce

Serves 4–5 | Time taken: 30 minutes

Carrots are the basic ingredient in this dish, but it is the rich béchamel sauce that gives it flavour. The sauce is creamy yet not so smooth as to prevent the various spicy ingredients from being tasted. A nice contrast to the rather plain carrots.

1 520 g (1 lb 2½ oz) tin small whole carrots

For the sauce:
25 g (1 oz) butter
1 tablespoon flour
300 ml (½ pint)
1 heaped tablespoon parsley, finely chopped
1 heaped tablespoon capers, finely ground
3–4 gherkins, finely chopped
milk and carrot juice mixed
salt to taste, and freshly milled black pepper

Drain the liquid from the tin of carrots into a bowl. Put the carrots into a medium-sized, shallow oven dish, that will accommodate them and also allow the sauce to cover them completely. Put the dish to one side.

Preheat oven to 190°C, 375°F or Gas No. 5.

Now prepare the sauce. First make the roux: melt the butter in a saucepan, stir in the flour carefully and remove from heat. Add a little of the milk and carrot liquid, mix well until smooth and return saucepan to heat. Gradually stir in the rest of the liquid. Throw in the parsley, capers and gherkins and plenty of pepper and taste before adding salt – it may need very little. Cook on a low heat for two minutes, stirring gently all the time.

Pour the sauce over the carrots and warm up in the hot oven for 10–15 minutes. Serve with fish, and plain boiled rice or potatoes.

Leeks in tomato sauce

Serves 4 | Time taken: 30 minutes

This is a hot vegetable dish full of goodness and nourishment which can be served with either fish or chicken. When buying leeks pick out the tight slim ones and those with the longest white stalks as they'll be easier to clean.

5 leeks
1 396 (14 oz) tin tomatoes
115 g (4 oz) hard Danish blue cheese, grated
3–4 garlic cloves, crushed
salt and freshly milled black pepper

Clean the leeks thoroughly and cut them in half lengthwise. Put them in a saucepan, cover them with salted water and bring to the boil. Cook for a while (the time will depend on size and freshness) but do not overcook as they are not nice soggy. Drain well in a colander then place them in a shallow ovenproof dish and set aside.

Preheat oven to 200°C, 400°F or Gas No. 6.

Empty the tin of tomatoes into an electric blender and liquidize for a few seconds. Pour out into a mixing bowl, add the cheese, the garlic and pepper and salt to taste. Mix well and pour over the leeks. place in the oven and bake for 15 minutes.

Rice with lentils

Serves 10–12 Time taken: 15 minutes

1 396 g (14 oz) tin boiled lentils
2 large spanish onions
5 tablespoons oil
150 ml (¼ pint) boiling water
2 260 (9¼ oz) tins Uncle Ben's 'heat'n' serve' rice
1 teaspoon salt

You will need a medium-sized saucepan for this recipe. Drain the tin of lentils in a colander then swirl cold water over them and let them stand. Finely chop one onion and fry in the hot oil until golden brown, then stir in the lentils: do not fry for longer than 3 minutes as they are already quite soft. Pour the boiling water into the pan, adding the salt and then the rice. Stir the mixture well and cook with the lid on for about three minutes.

In the meantime, finely slice the other onion and fry in a little oil until brown. Now tip the rice and lentils into a serving dish and arrange the fried onion over it.

Red cabbage with apple

Serves 4–6 Time taken: 15 minutes

This is a versatile dish which can be eaten hot or cold. It is the addition of fresh sliced apples and soured cream which makes it particularly appealing.

540 g (1 lb 3 oz) tin red cabbage, with apples if possible
2 medium-sized green eating apples
2–3 spring onions, finely chopped
1–2 142 ml (5 fl oz) cartons soured cream
lemon juice (optional)

If you decide to eat this dish hot, prepare it in a saucepan and simply heat it up. Use a nice salad bowl if you wish to have it cold. Put the well-drained cabbage in the bowl. Peel, core and cut the apples into quarters, then slice them finely. Add to the cabbage, followed by the onion, and the soured cream. If you feel really extravagant use two cartons of soured cream. Toss salad thoroughly.

Stuffed cabbage leaves with cumin rice and tomato sauce

Serves 10–12

Preparation time: 40 minutes
Cooking time: 1 hour

Unlike the filling on p. 52 this recipe contains no meat and is ideal for vegetarians.

For the sauce:
150 ml (¼ pint) oil
1 large onion, finely sliced
1 garlic clove, finely sliced
2 140 g (5 oz) tins tomato purée
600 ml (1 pint) boiling water
2 tablespoons Worcestershire sauce
1 teaspoon dried mixed herbs
salt and freshly milled black pepper

For the stuffing:
25 level teaspoons uncooked rice (allow roughly 1 teaspoon per leaf)
2 tablespoons oil
1 tomato, peeled and chopped
1 dessertspoon parsley, chopped
2 teaspoons cumin seed
salt and freshly milled black pepper

1 large green cabbage (2–3 lbs)

Start by making the tomato sauce. In a little of the oil fry the onion and garlic until lightly brown and add the tomato purée. Gradually stir in the boiling water, the Worcestershire sauce, the herbs and the salt and pepper. Add the rest of the oil slowly, stirring all the time and simmer for 15 minutes or so.

Now wash the cabbage and trim the stalk, discard the damaged leaves and drop the cabbage in boiling salted water. Cook for 8–15 minutes or until the leaves peel off easily – the time will depend on how tender the cabbage is. Put in a colander to drain (but do not throw away the boiled water) and swill a little cold water over the cabbage or it will be too hot to handle.

Set the oven to 180°C, 350°F or Gas No. 4.

In a mixing bowl mix the ingredients together for the stuffing. Pull off the cabbage leaves one by one and if the inner ones do not come away easily return cabbage to the boil for a few minutes. Dry them a little and then, using scissors, snip out the hardest part of the stalk at the base of each leaf. Put about a teaspoon of the rice mixture into each leaf. Tuck the sides in first, then roll up tight. When all the leaves have been stuffed pack them side by side and close together in an ovenproof dish and sprinkle them with salt. Pour the tomato sauce over them, cover with foil and cook for 1 hour. The sauce should more or less cover the cabbage during cooking time, so add a little boiling water if necessary – it won't matter as the sauce will be quite thick anyway.

Risotto with peas and tomato sauce

Serves 4–5 Time taken: 20 minutes

You'll have no work to do for this recipe as all the ingredients come from tins. Tins lend themselves very well to the cooking of risotto as this dish should be creamy and soft.

1 260 g (9¼ oz) tin Uncle Ben's 'heat'n' serve' rice
25 g (1 oz) butter
1 375 g (13¼ oz) tin tomato and onion sauce (sometimes labelled Cook-in-Sauce)
1 283 g (10 oz) tin small peas
generous sprinkle of grated Parmesan cheese

Cook the rice according to the instructions on the tin, adding the butter at the same time. When the rice is ready, tip contents of the tin of sauce into the pan and stir. (There will be a little too much sauce, so discard a couple of tablespoons before pouring.) Cook for 10 minutes, then add the drained peas. Cook with the lid off and on a high heat until the sauce has been absorbed into the rice but do not allow it to dry up as this dish should be eaten quite moist. Turn out on to a serving dish and sprinkle generously with Parmesan cheese.

Desserts

You can really go to town with desserts as tinned fruit provides great scope for a marvellous variety of appealing recipes. Included here are some unusual combinations such as 'Cranberry and Cider', 'Prunes and Honey', and 'Grapes in Yogurt'; there are more common but equally delicious puddings like 'Plum Charlotte' or 'Apricot Tart'. As well as desserts based on packets and jars we've also included biscuit- and sponge-based desserts and some made with ready-made pastry. Because of the large variety of sponge mixes available we have suggested various fillings which might come in handy for entertaining to tea or coffee. A number of fillings for sweet pancakes (savoury ones will be found in another section) are included as there are several brands of pancake mixes and they are just as good as anything home-made.

Wherever possible we have separated the actual time spent making the dessert and the time allowed for baking or chilling. This is particularly helpful with desserts since they constitute the last course in a meal. It means that one can carefully work out the menu and be sure that the dessert is ready on time.

Tins of fruit come in a wider variety of sizes than meat or fish and it was often tempting to cater for larger numbers using king-size tins. For the most part, however, we decided to use the tin with the average number of helpings and simply point out when the recipe could be made in larger quantities. With experience, you will easily be able to vary the quantities for yourself. So, whether you're in a hurry or have time in hand, whether you're in the mood for a light and refreshing mousse or a rich and more substantial dessert, you should find something here to suit you.

Marmalade roly poly with honey syrup

Serves 6–8

Preparation time: 15–20 minutes
Baking time: 30–40 minutes

This is an easy dessert to prepare, a delicious addition to the family's Sunday tea table. It would be particularly welcome on cold winter days.

1 packet 454 g (1 lb) short pastry
⅓ tin of 907 g (2 lb) Seville orange marmalade
2 tablespoons honey
¼ teaspoon ground cloves
½ teaspoon orange essence
4–5 tablespoons boiling water

Sprinkle the working surface with flour. Cut the pastry into two lots so it will be easier to handle: making two roly polies will reduce the size of baking tray needed. Now roll each piece of pastry until fairly thin but not thin enough to fall apart.

Preheat oven to 190°C, 380°F or Gas No. 5.

Take two thirds of the marmalade and spread evenly over the pastry, then roll it up like a Swiss roll and prick holes along the top for decoration and also to allow steam to escape during baking.

Put the roly poly on to a greased tray and into the hot oven for 30–40 minutes or until light brown.

Whilst the pastry is baking make the sauce: put the remaining marmalade into a small saucepan, add the honey, cloves and orange essence. Add the water gradually, stirring well. Be sure no lumps are left. Bring to the boil and cook for 2–3 minutes. Pour the hot sauce over the roly poly.

Different varieties of jam such as raspberry or strawberry, can be used instead of marmalade, only make sure the essence and spices are adapted accordingly because jams have a more delicate flavour than marmalade.

Roly poly with hot marmalade sauce

Serves 6–8 Time taken: 35 minutes

A welcome dessert or a tea-time treat for cold winter days.

1 454 g (1 lb) packet short pastry
6 tablespoons marmalade (coarse or fine)
pinch of ground cloves or mixed spice
4–6 tablespoons water
4 tablespoons sherry

Preheat oven to 190°C, 375°F or Gas No. 5.

Cover your working surface with flour and roll out the pastry. Spread four tablespoons of the marmalade over the pastry, roll it up, prick it with a fork along the top and bake in the hot oven for 20 minutes.

Whilst the pastry is in the oven, make the sauce. Put the remaining two tablespoons of marmalade, the spice, and the water into a small saucepan, mix well and cook for a few minutes, stirring continuously. Add the sherry, stir again, and cook for another few minutes.

Pour the sauce over the pastry and serve hot.

Apricot meringue

Serves 5–6

Time taken: 25 minutes

1 375 g (13¼ oz) sweetened ready-cooked apricots
2 tablespoons water
2 142 ml (5 fl oz) cartons double cream
1 packet meringue mix (they often contain 5 sachets so one sachet should be enough)
140 g (5 oz) sugar usually required to make the meringue

Mix the apricots and water together and liquidize to a rough consistency – there should be lots of apricot bits in the mixture. Whisk the cream until thick, then fold in the apricot purée. Pour into a pie dish.

Read the instructions on the packet carefully and set the oven to the right temperature. Now make the meringue – sugar and water are normally required – then cover the apricot mixture with it. Baking should take about 10 minutes or until the meringue is brown.

Apricot and orange dessert

Serves 8–10

Time taken: 40 minutes

This lovely rich dessert is ideal for a large dinner party.

454 g (1 lb) dried apricots (soaked overnight in water)
2 tablespoons sugar
1 large orange with thin rind if possible
300 ml (½ pint) double cream
a little Grand Marnier if desired

If you have not anticipated making this dessert and have not soaked the apricots the night before, you can still make the recipe but you'll have to allow a bit longer for the apricots to soften. Cover the apricots with water in a saucepan, add the sugar and the thinly sliced orange with the peel on. Simmer for about 30 minutes or until the apricots are quite soft. Let fruit cool down for a while then purée in a blender.

Whip the cream (leaving a little aside for decoration) and add the Grand Marnier if desired. Now fold the apricot purée into the cream and pour the mixture into individual dishes. Decorate with the reserved cream and put in the fridge to cool.

Hot apricot dessert

Serves 4–5

Time taken: 35 minutes

Dried and ready-cooked apricots in packets have a great deal of flavour and can therefore be used in a variety of ways to provide excellent desserts. The kind of apricots recommended for this recipe need no preparation at all and can be used at once.

- 4 egg whites
- ¾ teaspoon vanilla flavouring essence
- 2 tablespoons castor sugar
- 1 375 g (13¼ oz) packet sweetened ready-cooked apricots
- juice of 1 lemon

Preheat the oven to 190°C, 375°F or Gas No. 5.
Put the egg whites in a mixing bowl and add the vanilla flavouring. Beat with an electric mixer and when stiff gradually incorporate the castor sugar. Continue beating for a few seconds.

Now purée the apricots together with the lemon juice in a blender or a sieve but make sure it retains a thick and rough consistency and does not become smooth and runny. Fold the apricot purée into the egg whites. Line a soufflé dish with greaseproof paper and pour the mixture into it. Bake for 20 minutes or until the top is golden brown. This dessert should be light and mousse-like and must not be allowed to overcook. Serve straight away.

Apricot tart

Serves 6–8

Preparation time: 20 minutes
Setting time: 1½ hours

- 400 g (14 oz) standard packet digestive biscuits
- 225 g (8 oz) butter (taken out of the fridge early to soften)
- 820 g (1 lb 13 oz) tin apricot halves in syrup
- 2 level teaspoons gelatine
- 4 tablespoons cold water
- 1 tablespoon marmalade
- 1 tablespoon brandy
- fresh cream

Crumble the biscuits and blend with the butter (it helps if a wooden crusher is used). Carry on until biscuits and butter are blended into an even crumb mixture. Fill a large tart dish of 30 cm (12 in) diameter, with the crumbled biscuits pressing down hard to pack the biscuits in tightly. Use the rounded side of a wooden spoon or end of a rounded mallet to help.

Take apricots out of tin (reserving the syrup for later) and arrange them – rounded side up – on top of the biscuits. Try to cover the surface evenly and fully.

Now mix the gelatine with the four spoons of cold water in a cup or a bowl and then put it into a saucepan of boiling water. Place on a medium heat, stirring the gelatine until it dissolves properly. Take the bowl out of the saucepan and all the gelatine to cool for a few minutes. Pour it into the apricot syrup, stir well, add the marmalade and mix it in.

Pour the brandy over the apricots and then pour the prepared syrup and gelatine over the tart. Leave for 1½ hours to allow the gelatine to set around the apricots. Serve with fresh cream.

Apricot and lychee special

Serves 6–8 Time taken: 35 minutes

This is an attractive dessert and one special enough to make for a celebration or an important occasion.

3 eggs, separated
75 g (3 oz) icing sugar
50 g (2 oz) butter
300 ml (½ pint) double cream
2 425 g (15 oz) tins apricot halves
2 teaspoons (1 sachet) gelatine
1–2 tablespoons Kirsch
1 340 g (12 oz) tin lychees, drained
12 round ginger biscuits

To prepare this dessert you will need three small bowls. Beat the egg yolks, the sugar and butter in one of them, until the mixture is smooth and thick. Beat the egg whites in the second bowl until stiff. Then, in the third bowl, whip the cream to a thick but not stiff consistency. Put the three bowls to one side.

Purée the apricots (leaving a few for decoration) in a liquidizer, then put 4 tablespoons of the purée in a saucepan. On a very low heat, dissolve the gelatine in it, stirring continuously but without bringing the mixture to the boil. When the gelatine is well dissolved, take off the heat, let the mixture cool down for a few minutes, then stir in the rest of the puréed apricots.

Now add the prepared egg mixture, the egg whites, half the cream and the Kirsch to the apricot purée. Stir in the lychees very gently (leaving a few for decoration) to prevent them from breaking. Put the mixture into a round mould with a hollow centre and put in the freezer to set for 20 minutes.

When it has set turn it out on to a round dish with an edge about 5 cm (2 in) high (or roughly the size of the biscuits). Place the biscuits upright round the moulded dessert and fill the centre with the reserved lychees and the drained apricots. Decorate with the rest of the cream.

Apricots with soured cream

Serves 4 | Time taken: 10 minutes

1 411 g (14½ oz) tin apricot halves, drained
2 heaped tablespoons vanilla sugar
1 142 ml (5 fl oz) carton soured cream
2 heaped tablespoons blanched and sliced almonds

Arrange the apricots on a shallow serving dish with the rounded side up. Sprinkle the sugar through a sieve over them.

Beat the soured cream lightly and pour it over the apricots. Sprinkle with almonds and serve chilled.

Prunes and honey dessert

Serves 4–6 | Time taken: 15 minutes

1 425 g (15 oz) tin prunes in syrup
1 level tablespoon cornflour
25 g (1 oz) butter
2 tablespoons honey
2 egg whites

Strain the liquid from the tin of prunes into a small bowl. While the prunes are in the strainer remove the stones and then mash the prunes in an electric blender for a few seconds. If you have no blender available use a hand mixer or mash with a fork through a large strainer. It will take a bit longer and you must be careful not to leave any lumps.

In a small saucepan dissolve the cornflour in a little prune juice. Make sure that no lumps are left and then add the remaining juice; stir again and bring the liquid gently to the boil. Keep stirring continuously until the liquid thickens. Take the pan off the heat, add the butter and the honey letting them dissolve in the liquid before adding the prune purée.

Leave the mixture to cool.

Beat the egg whites in a separate bowl until stiff and fold into the prune mixture. Serve chilled.

Orange and mandarin special

Serves 3 | Time taken: 20 minutes

1 large orange
1 312 g (11 oz) tin mandarins in syrup
50 g (2 oz) castor sugar
2 tablespoons water
fresh cream

Remove the outer rind of the orange with a sharp knife and cut it into thin matchstick strips. Put the strips into a saucepan, just covering with water. Bring to the boil and cook for 5–7 minutes. Drain off the hot water and rinse the strips in cold running water. Then put them to one side.

After removing the pith from the orange, cut it into thin slices, discarding any pips. Arrange the slices at the bottom of a glass dish. Now drain off the syrup from the mandarins and put it to one side. Arrange the mandarin segments on top of the orange slices. Finally put the strips of peel over the mandarins.

And now make the caramel. Put the sugar in a small saucepan and pour in the water. Let the sugar dissolve slowly over a gentle heat. When dissolved increase the heat and boil until the syrup becomes thick and brownish. Remove the pan from the heat and immediately pour in the syrup from the mandarins. Let it harden, then crush the caramel inside the saucepan with a spoon and sprinkle it over the oranges.

Serve with lashings of fresh cream.

Orange juice and blackberry frost

Serves 6–8

Time taken to prepare: 15 minutes
Time taken to set: 20 minutes
Time taken to chill: 20 minutes

600 ml (1 pint) orange juice from carton or tin
1 219 g (7¾ oz) tin blackberries in syrup
2 teaspoons (1 packet) powdered gelatine
4 tablespoons cold water
1 170 g (6 oz) tin Nestle's cream
1 egg white

Blend the orange juice and the contents of the tin of blackberries in an electric blender for a few seconds. Put the gelatine with the water into a small bowl and place in a saucepan of boiling water and boil until the gelatine dissolves completely, stirring all the time. Take the bowl out of the saucepan and allow to cool for two minutes. Then pour the gelatine into the electric blender and blend with the other ingredients for a few minutes.

Pour the mixture out of the blender into a bowl and put it into the freezer to set for 20 minutes. During that time drain the excess liquid off the cream, put the cream into a bowl and whisk until light. In another bowl beat the egg white until stiff. When the mixture in the freezer begins to thicken, fold in first the cream and then the egg white. Blend all the ingredients very gently and put into the refrigerator to set further and chill well.

Pears with chocolate fudge

Serves 4

Time taken: 25 minutes

1 820 g (1 lb 13 oz) pear halves in syrup
2 tablespoons crushed almonds
For the fudge:
226 g (8 oz) castor sugar
4 tablespoons pear juice
1 level tablespoon golden syrup
25 g (1 oz) unsalted butter
25 g (1 oz) cocoa

Drain the pears thoroughly but keep 4 tablespoons of juice for later. It's worth taking a few extra minutes over this because any liquid that remains will only make the fudge runny. Remember too that tinned pears are delicate so handle them carefully to make sure they do not break. Once they are well drained arrange the pears in a serving dish with the scooped side underneath. Scatter the crushed almonds over them and put the dish to one side.

Now make the fudge, which is thick and scrumptuous. Put all the ingredients in a small, heavy-bottomed saucepan and place the pan on a low heat stirring continuously until the butter has dissolved and all the ingredients are well blended. Once the mixture begins to bubble reduce the heat to a minimum and simmer for 10 minutes. You will find the sauce reduces in quantity as it thickens. During the ten minutes of simmering do not stir continuously as this will cause the fudge icing to grain, but from time to time draw a wooden spoon through the mixture to see whether it has thickened enough.

Remove the pan from the heat. Leave to cool for a while then pour over the pears. Serve chilled.

Crème de marrons

Serves 4–6

Time taken: 15 minutes

Here is a recipe for chestnut lovers and one which will go down well with your guests. It's economical too as a small tin will go a long way.

1 142 ml (5 fl oz) carton double cream
1 250 g (8¾ oz) tin chestnut purée
3 egg whites
4–5 brandy snaps, crushed macaroons (optional)

In a mixing bowl whip the cream until thick but not stiff, add the chestnut purée and mix well. Beat the egg whites in an electric mixer or by hand and fold them into the mixture. Put into a serving dish and into the refrigerator to cool. Before serving, sprinkle the crushed brandy snaps on top. Alternatively, or in addition, arrange macaroons on a plate and hand round separately.

Chestnut dessert

Serves 6–8 Time taken: 20 minutes

A really delicious dish. As the quantity is considerable it is ideal for summer parties. If the opportunity is not there to use it all at once it can be kept in the freezer and served on several occasions.

1 454 g (1 lb) tin natural chestnut purée
115 g (4 oz) icing sugar
1 tablespoon honey
½ teaspoon vanilla essence
1 tablespoon rum
300 ml (½ pint) double cream

Combine the chestnut purée, sugar and honey in a mixing bowl. Mix gently by hand or with an electric mixer on the lowest speed until the mixture is smooth and even. At this stage add the vanilla and rum. Now in a separate bowl beat the cream until thick but not stiff and fold it into the chestnut mixture. Transfer into a decorative serving bowl and put into a freezer to cool for about 10 minutes.

Chestnuts and chocolate purée

Serves 4–6 Time taken: 20 minutes

An electric handbeater could be very useful in preparing this recipe, otherwise use a hand whisk or fork.

1 440 g (15½ oz) tin chestnut purée (unsweetened)
2 tablespoons thick honey
2 heaped tablespoons cocoa powder
170 g (6 oz) Nestle's cream
½ teaspoon lemon juice (optional)
1 tablespoon grated chocolate or decorative chocolate drops

Blend the chestnut purée and honey well together. Add the cocoa powder gradually by putting through a flour sieve or coffee strainer. Drain the liquid off the tinned cream and beat lightly before adding the chestnut mixture. Add a little lemon juice if required and whisk for a few seconds. Transfer the purée into a serving dish and put it in a refrigerator to set and cool for about 15 minutes. Before serving sprinkle the grated chocolate over the top.

Compôte supreme

Serves 12–14 Time taken: 10 minutes

This compôte of berries is really supreme in every way. It has a tangy, sharp flavour and the different kinds of berries together with the oranges make it particularly appealing to the eye. It is ideal for a summer's day, served chilled and with cream.

Making this compôte for only a few people is hardly worthwhile because several large tins have to be used to get the proportions right. It is truly a party recipe.

- 5–6 medium-sized oranges
- 454 g (16 oz) tin bilberries in syrup
- 410 g (14½ oz) tin Cape loganberries in syrup
- 500 g (18 oz) jar or tin cherries in syrup
- 212 g (7½ oz) tin blackberries
- lemon or sugar (optional)
- fresh cream

Peel the oranges. Remove the pith. With a sharp knife on a wooden board, slice them into very thin rings, removing the pips whilst cutting. Put the orange slices into a serving bowl and place the contents of the tins on top – the order is not important. Mix very gently, so as not to break some of the more delicate fruit, and taste. The proportions and combination of fruit given here should suit most tastes but if the compôte seems tart, add a little sugar, if too sweet add lemon juice. When serving make sure that a little of every fruit is included in each dish.

Serve with fresh cream.

Strawberry crème de la crème

Serves 4–6 Time taken: 15 minutes

This dessert looks very attractive served in individual dishes, ones which allow the coloured layers to be visible. Have the dishes standing by, so that the ingredients can be poured into them individually.

- 2 egg whites
- 1–2 tablespoons castor sugar
- 1 tablespoon lemon juice
- 1–2 drops lemon essence
- 1 strawberry yogurt – with real fruit in it
- 1 heaped tablespoon of strawberry jam – with whole fruit in it
- 142 ml (5 fl oz) double cream
- 4–6 fresh strawberries to decorate

Start by beating the egg whites. When they are nearly stiff put in the sugar, add the lemon juice and the lemon essence. Continue beating for a few more minutes so that the sugar is dissolved and the lemon juice well blended in. When ready, divide the mixture equally between the individual dishes.

Blend the yogurt and jam in an electric blender for a few minutes to ensure a complete mix. Pour this mixture on to the egg white base in each dish.

Next beat the cream until thick but not stiff. Decorate the top of each dish with the cream using a cream piper or corner of a greaseproof bag to make a pattern. Place a fresh strawberry in the centre of each dish. Serve chilled.

Raspberry cream dessert

Serves 4–6

Time taken: 12 minutes

This delicious dessert is quick and easy to make and is ideal for a summer party.

1 60 g (2¼ oz) raspberry flavour dessert mix
300 ml (½ pint) milk
1 170 g (6 oz) Nestle's cream
1 teaspoon lemon juice
½ teaspoon lemon flavouring
1 egg
honey or syrup to decorate

Pour the dessert mix into a bowl, stir in the milk, beat gently, and put aside for a while.

Pour out all the excess water from the tin of cream and using an electric mixer beat until light and fluffy. Add the lemon juice and lemon flavouring to the cream and whip for a few more seconds. Beat in the egg until creamy and combine with the dessert mix stirring gently but thoroughly. Fill individual dishes and decorate with swirls of honey or syrup before serving.

Apple and raspberry jam pancakes

Serves 4

Time taken: 20 minutes

1 127 g (4½ oz) packet lemon-flavoured pancake mix (which requires the addition of 1 egg)
For the filling:
1 383 g (13½ oz) tin apple slices
2 dessertspoons sugar (if apples unsweetened)
juice of ½ lemon
5 dessertspoons raspberry jam
generous pinch of cinnamon

Make the pancakes according to the instructions on the packet and pile them flat on a plate as you go along.

Put the apple slices in a bowl together with the sugar, the lemon juice, 2 tablespoons of raspberry jam (keep the rest for the topping) and the cinnamon. Mix the ingredients thoroughly then fill each pancake with some of the mixture and place them in a greased baking tray. Using a knife spread the rest of the raspberry jam on the pancakes before putting them under the grill for 5–10 minutes.

Raspberry delight

Serves 4–5 Time taken: 15 minutes

This dessert is not only delicious it also looks very attractive and appetizing, especially if served in a glass dish.

2 egg whites
284 ml (10 fl oz) double cream
4 dessertspoons sugar
1 425 g (15 oz) tin raspberries in syrup
juice of ½ lemon

Beat the egg whites until stiff. In a separate bowl whip the cream with half the sugar until fairly thick but not stiff. Fold the cream (leaving a little aside for decorating later) into the egg whites. Then, using a fork, mash the drained raspberries to a pulp and stir in the lemon juice and the rest of the sugar. Now mix all the ingredients together, pour into a serving bowl and decorate with the reserved cream. Whirl this into the mixture with the help of a fork so that it leaves a decorative white trail. Cool before serving.

Blackcurrants in cream

Serves 3–4 Time taken: 10 minutes

This rather rich dessert is particularly appealing because tinned blackcurrants are firm. It is ideal for topping ice cream or sorbet.

1 213 g (7½ oz) tin blackcurrants
300 ml (½ pint) double cream
a squeeze of lemon and sugar (optional)

Separate the blackcurrants from their juice, keeping the blackcurrants in the tin. In a medium-sized bowl beat the cream until it is thick but not too thick. Fold in the blackcurrants and add the lemon and sugar to taste. Serve chilled and pour a little of the juice over each portion or in the bowl.

Blackberries and lemon jelly dessert

Serves 4–5

Preparation time: 10 minutes
Setting time: 30 minutes

This dessert only takes 10 minutes to prepare but you must allow half an hour or so for it to set in the fridge. If you have a freezer, though, it will obviously be quicker – but you can always start your meal and by the time you get round to the pudding the jelly should have set.

1 215 g (7½ oz) tin blackberries
1 135 g (4¾ oz) packet lemon-flavoured jelly
300 ml (½ pint) blackberry juice and boiling water mixed together
a little sugar to taste
1 142 ml (5 fl oz) carton double cream
whipped cream to decorate (optional)

Drain the blackberries of their juice and pour the juice into a measuring jug. Then add the required amount of boiling water to make up half a pint. Break up the jelly with your hands and drop the pieces into a liquidizer, pour the liquid in and blend on a very high speed for a couple of minutes or until the jelly has properly dissolved. Now add the blackberries – reserving a few for decoration – a little sugar and the cream and blend for a few seconds. Pour into a bowl or individual glasses, scatter the reserved blackberries over the top and decorate with a little whipped cream if desired. Chill or freeze until the dessert is firm but not stiff.

Blackberry fluff

Serves 4–6

Preparation time: 5 minutes
Setting time: up to 2 hours

1 packet blackcurrant jelly
1 213 g (7½ oz) tin blackberries
water

Read the instructions on the jelly packet as to how to make it. Use the juice of blackberries instead of water and if the liquid is not sufficient add some water. Put the jelly to set into the freezer. Then take it out and put it into an electric blender for about 2 minutes or until the jelly has changed to a pale milky pink colour. Pour out into a shallow serving dish or individual dishes and put back into the refrigerator to cool and set.

Serve on its own with ice cream or tinned fruit.

Cherry clafoutis

Serves 6–7

Preparation time: 15 minutes
Baking time: 45 minutes

This is a delicious but rather extravagant dessert which will use up a lot of your basic ingredients but is well worth a try.

4 eggs
2 egg yolks
pinch of salt
125 g (4½ oz) castor sugar
100 g (3½ oz) plain flour
50 g (2 oz) butter
600 ml (1 pint) milk
½ teaspoon vanilla essence
1 425 g (15 oz) tin black cherries

Preheat the oven to 180°C, 350°F or Gas No. 4.
Beat all the eggs and the pinch of salt first for a few seconds, then add the sugar and beat until the mixture is creamy. Gradually incorporate the sifted flour and beat continuously until smooth and free from lumps. Now melt half the butter in a small pan and add it to the

mixing bowl followed by the milk and the vanilla essence. Beat for a few more seconds, then stir in the drained cherries but keep the juice for later.

Pour the mixture into a soufflé dish, dot with the rest of the butter and bake for 45 minutes. The top should by then be crisp and golden and the inside moist and creamy. Sprinkle with castor sugar and serve straight away. Hand the cherry juice round separately to pour over the pudding.

Cranberries and cider dessert

Serves 6–8

Time to prepare: 15 minutes
Time to set: 30 minutes

If after a lunch you find yourself left with half a jar of cranberries and some sparkling wine, here is a perfect dessert to make for dinner. The cranberries in this recipe are those usually served with meat. They are of extra good quality and flavour.

- half of 425 g (15 oz) jar cranberries
- 300 ml (½ pint) orange juice from carton or tin
- 1 teaspoon powdered gelatine
- 2 tablespoons water
- 300 ml (½ pint) cider or sparkling wine
- fresh double cream

Put the cranberries and orange juice into an electric blender for two minutes or until the mixture is smooth and without lumps. Leave for a while.

Put the gelatine and water into a small bowl and into a saucepan with boiling water. Boil the water until the gelatine dissolves, stirring all the time. Take out the bowl and leave to cool for a few minutes. When cooled add to the mixture in the blender together with the wine and blend for another few seconds.

Pour into a serving dish and put into the refrigerator to set and cool for 30 minutes. Serve with a dollop of cream.

Plum charlotte

Serves 4–6 Time taken: 30 minutes

A really excellent Plum Charlotte can be made with Victoria plums as they are particularly tasty.

170 g (6 oz) fresh white breadcrumbs
2 567 g (1 lb 4 oz) tins Victoria plums in syrup
50 g (2 oz) butter
50 g (2 oz) soft brown sugar and 25 g (1 oz) cinnamon mixed together

Set your oven to 220°C, 425°F or Gas No. 7.
For the breadcrumbs use sliced bread (cut the crusts off) put into a liquidizer for a few seconds. Set them aside for a few minutes. Drain the plums but keep the juice as you'll need some of it. Butter the bottom and sides of a soufflé dish or a similar ovenproof dish (it should be deep but not too wide). Then spread some of the breadcrumbs followed by 3–4 tablespoons of plum juice, the lemon juice and a little of the mixed brown sugar and cinnamon. Place some of the plums over them and continue to build up the layers using the breadcrumbs, the syrup, dots of butter, sugar, cinnamon and the lemon juice, then the plums again until all the ingredients have been used up. Finish off with a layer of breadcrumbs dotted with bits of butter and a final sprinkle of sugar and cinnamon. Bake for 15–20 minutes or until the top is golden brown.

Plums and apple crumble

Serves 4 Time taken: 25 minutes

This recipe is extremely simple – it is the combination of the two tins which makes it rather special.

1 383 g ($13\frac{1}{2}$ oz) tin apple slices
2 teaspoons brown sugar
sprinkle of cinnamon
1 567 g (1 lb 4 oz) tin red plums
juice of 1 lemon
1 227 g (8 oz) packet crumble mix

Preheat oven to 200°C, 400°F or Gas No. 6.
Place the apple slices in a suitable pie dish and sprinkle with some sugar and cinnamon. Add the red plums together with three tablespoons of the juice and the lemon juice. Scatter cinnamon and sugar over them then cover with the crumble and top with a little sugar and cinnamon. Bake for 20 minutes or until golden brown.

Peach tart

Serves 5 Time taken: 20–25 minutes

For this recipe a 454 g (1 lb) packet of shortcrust pastry mix has to be used since most packets currently on the market come in roughly that quantity. To make this tart, however, you will only need about 227 g (8 oz) to fill a 22 cm (9 in) fluted flan tin and preferably one with a loose base. If you are not using the rest of the mix immediately be sure to keep it in an airtight bag or container or use all the packet up and store the dough in the fridge.

227 g (8 oz) shortcrust pastry mix
1 410 g (14½ oz) tin peach halves in syrup
1 35 g (1¼ oz) packet orange jelly glaze
1 dessertspoon crushed almonds
1 teaspoon cinnamon
2 dessertspoons sugar

Read the instructions on the packet of pastry mix and set the oven at the right temperature. Grease the flan tin. Mix the pastry with the required amount of water (we used 2 tablespoons) and work the pastry into a round ball with your fingertips. Now roll it out with a rolling pin on a floured surface then line the flan tin with the pastry using your fingers to spread it evenly. Prick the dough all over with a fork and bake for the required time – it will take about 20 minutes.

Now turn to the peaches and the glaze: drain the peaches but keep the syrup and use it to produce the right amount of liquid required to make the glaze. Usually 200 ml (7 fl oz) of liquid is required but read the instructions on the packet first and then proceed as directed. Blend the cinnamon in a little water before adding it to the thickening glaze then stir in the almonds and the sugar to taste. Remove the tart from the oven and allow it to cool for a little while before taking it out of the tin. Sprinkle with sugar and place the peach halves (inside part down) on the tart and evenly spread the glaze over them and between them. Leave to set for a few minutes and serve with cream if desired.

Peaches and cream dessert

Serves 4–6 Time taken: 5 minutes

This dessert can be made in a few minutes and is ideal if a large number of people descend on you.

1 410 g (14½ oz) tin peach halves
1 142 ml (5 fl oz) carton double cream
½ teaspoon lemon flavouring

Liquidize the contents of the tin of peaches in an electric blender for a few seconds. In a separate bowl beat the cream until fairly thick but not stiff. Now blend the two together, add the flavouring and mix gently until an even mixture is obtained. Put in the refrigerator to chill before serving.

Apple fritters

Serves 7–8 Time taken: 20–25 minutes

If you want to use up most of the batter in this recipe you will need to use 2 tins of apples. But if you would rather be left with some batter to use either the next day or for another recipe, only use one tin.

For the batter:
115 g (4 oz) self-raising flour
¼ teaspoon salt
2 tablespoons sugar
1 egg
150 ml (¼ pint) milk

oil for frying
2 383 g (13½ oz) tins apple slices
pinch cinnamon
a little lemon
sprinkle of sugar

Sift the flour and salt into a mixing bowl then add the sugar. Make a well in the centre, put the egg in and gradually stir in half the milk. Mix vigorously for a few minutes then incorporate the rest of the milk and go on beating until the mixture is smooth.

Turn on your grill to a medium heat.

Get a large frying pan out and cover the bottom with oil. As fritters should be served as soon as they are ready, it is important to use a large pan so that the apples can be fried in no more than two batches. Empty the contents of the tins into a bowl and separate the apples with a fork. Sprinkle generously with cinnamon. To save time and because tinned apples are small, use a slotted spoon to dip them in the batter rather than dipping them individually. Coat them well and put into the hot oil but spread them out so that they do not stick together. As the apple slices are soft wait until one side is crisp and firm before turning them over. Drain well on absorbent kitchen paper and arrange in a nice ovenproof dish before putting them under the grill to keep warm while you fry the second batch.

Before serving squeeze a little lemon over them and sprinkle with sugar.

Apple snow

Serves 4

Time taken: 10 minutes

1 383 g (13½ oz) tin apple slices (unsweetened)
2 tablespoons granulated sugar
2 tablespoons lemon juice
1 egg white
whipped cream to decorate

Put the apple slices together with the sugar in a liquidizer. Blend until the fruit has been broken up but do not allow it to become too runny – this dessert is so much nicer if you can taste pieces of apple. Add the lemon juice and pour the mixture into a bowl. Whisk the egg white until stiff then fold it into the apple mixture. Cool in a refrigerator for a while, then serve in individual glasses and top with a generous amount of whipped cream.

Apple and orange caramel

Serves 4–6

Time taken: 25–30 minutes

115 g (4 oz) sugar
150 ml (¼ pint) water
1 teaspoon vanilla essence
1 764 g (1 lb 11 oz) tin apple slices
2 large oranges

For the caramel:
75 g (3 oz) sugar
75 ml (3 fl oz) water

Put the sugar, water and vanilla essence into a saucepan, allowing the sugar to dissolve slowly over a gentle heat. When this has been done, turn up the heat and leave it on until the syrup is fairly thick. Now add the apple slices to the saucepan and shake the pan gently so that the apple slices separate but do not break. Simmer for 10 minutes then remove from the heat and cover with a lid. Now peel the oranges – setting aside the peel from one of them – slice them into thin rounds and remove all the pips. Then put the apples and the syrup into a large serving bowl and arrange the orange rounds on top.

Cut the peel which you set aside into thin matchstick strips. Put these in a small pan of water, bring to the boil and simmer for 5 minutes. Then drain and rinse in cold water and set aside.

To make the caramel put the sugar and water in a small pan and leave over a low heat until the liquid has turned to a rich brown colour. Pour into a greased shallow baking tin, sprinkle with the orange rind strips and leave to set. Then crush with a mallet or a rolling pin and sprinkle over the oranges. Serve chilled.

Lemon and apple pancakes

Serves 4 Time taken: 20 minutes

1 127 g (4½ oz) packet lemon-flavoured pancake mix
1 425 g (15 oz) tin apple purée
1 teaspoon lemon juice
1 teaspoon grated lemon rind

To make the pancakes, follow the instructions on the packet, but if you wish to make them extra tasty use half water and half milk when making the batter.

Mix the apple, lemon juice and rind to make the filling. Then spread a tablespoon of the mixture on to each pancake and roll it up. Continue doing this until both pancakes and filling have been used up. If there's some filling left over top the pancakes with the rest. Sprinkle with white or brown sugar and put in the oven to warm them up.

Gooseberry fool

Serves 4–6 Time taken: 15 minutes

This is a superb dessert which can be served after fish or meat.

1 552 g (1 lb 3½ oz) tin gooseberries in heavy syrup
2 teaspoons custard powder
150 ml (¼ pint) milk
142 ml (5 fl oz) double cream
½ teaspoon lemon flavouring

Drain off all liquid from the tin and keep. Rub the gooseberries through a sieve into a bowl but do not worry about lumps as they add flavour to this dessert. Now make the custard following the instructions on the tin or packet. Tip the custard into the bowl and stir gently. When the ingredients are well blended allow to cool.

Whip the cream until thick, then fold the gooseberry purée into it. Add the lemon flavouring and mix well. If the mixture is slightly thick, a little of the gooseberry syrup may be added.

Gooseberries and mango whip

Serves 6–8 Time taken: 25 minutes

It only takes 5 minutes to prepare this recipe but it needs to be in the refrigerator 15–20 minutes to set slightly and cool well. Gooseberries are usually tart and tinned mangoes rather sweet in flavour – they go well together.

1 383 g (13½ oz) tin Nestle's cream
1 283 g (10 oz) tin gooseberries in syrup
1 425 g (15 oz) tin sliced mangoes in syrup
4 drops lemon essence

Try to avoid shaking the tinned cream so that it will be easy to drain off the excess liquid. Having drained off as much liquid as possible, put the cream into a medium-sized bowl and beat it for a few minutes to make it lighter. Blend the contents of the tins of gooseberries and mangoes in an electric blender for a few minutes. Stop blending as soon as the two ingredients are well mixed – do not blend excessively. Then add the cream together with the essence drops to the mixture. Whisk lightly until the mixture is well blended, pour into serving dish and put it in the refrigerator to cool and set.

Gooseberry cheese cake dessert

Serves 6

Preparation time: 35 minutes
Cooling time: 15 minutes

This delicious cheesecake does not require baking and could be served as a dessert or for tea.

170 g (6 oz) muesli breakfast cereal
1 heaped tablespoon sultanas
300 ml (½ pint) double cream
50 g (2 oz) butter, melted
1 538 g (1 lb 3 oz) tin gooseberries in syrup, drained
1 tablespoon clear (from the bottle) lemon juice
50 g (2 oz) castor sugar
115 g (4 oz) cream cheese
1 142 g (5 fl oz) carton natural yogurt

Place the muesli and sultanas into a medium-sized flan dish. Moisten with a little of the cream and stir in the melted butter. When properly blended press the mixture tightly into the base of the dish and put it into the refrigerator while you get on with the rest of the preparations.

Mix the gooseberries, lemon juice and sugar in an electric blender for a few minutes.

In the meantime, beat the cream in a bowl until it begins to thicken, then add the cream cheese and yogurt, mix well and blend in the gooseberry purée. Now pour the mixture over the chilled muesli base, decorate if you wish with greated chocolate, and put back into the refrigerator to chill.

Grapes with yogurt

Serves 4–6

Time taken: 15–20 minutes

2 cartons pinapple yogurt
1 level teaspoon gelatine
2 tablespoons boiling water
1 411 g (14½ oz) seedless grapes in syrup
castor sugar if required

Put the yogurt in an electric blender for a few seconds so it becomes smooth.

Dissolve the gelatine in the boiling water, then add it to the yogurt in the liquidizer and blend for a second or two. Tip the mixture into a bowl, stir in the grapes and the syrup. Mix well and taste to see if additional sugar is required. Pour into a serving bowl or individual dishes and place in the refrigerator to set.

Blackberry mousse

Serves 4–6

Preparation time: 15 minutes
Setting time: 60 minutes

This is a light and refreshing dessert with an interesting seeded texture. Make it before the other courses as it needs at least an hour to set. In the summer children will love it instead of ice cream.

1 383 g (13½ oz) tin blackberries
2–3 tablespoons sugar
3 tablespoons cold water
1 teaspoon gelatine
1 142 ml (5 fl oz) carton double cream

Mix the contents of the tin of blackberries and the sugar in an electric blender for a few minutes, then set aside. Pour the water into a small basin and sprinkle the gelatine over it, then place it in a pan of hot water to dissolve slowly. Stir occasionally until the gelatine has dissolved and put aside to cool.

In the meantime, whip the cream until thick – but not stiff – in a mixing bowl large enough to accommodate all the ingredients. Now slowly fold the fruit mixture into the cream, followed by the cooled gelatine and mix thoroughly. Pour into a serving dish or individual bowls and put it in the refrigerator to set.

Mango mousse

Serves 4–5 Time taken: 30 minutes

If you like the delicate flavour of mangoes you will love this recipe.

- 1 410 g (14½ oz) tin of sliced mangoes
- 2 tablespoons sugar
- 2 teaspoons gelatine dissolved in 1½ tablespoons of boiling water
- 2 egg whites
- 2 142 ml (5 fl oz) cartons double cream

Blend together the sliced mangoes with two tablespoons of the juice and the sugar. Now dissolve the gelatine in the boiling water – it should be clear if it's well dissolved – and add to the blender. Liquidize well and on a high speed for a few minutes. Now beat the egg whites until they are stiff and thoroughly fold the mango mixture into it. Pour the mousse into a serving bowl and chill for 15 minutes or so in the coldest part of the fridge, or until it has stiffened slightly. Whip the cream lightly and swirl it into pretty patterns all over the mousse.

Tropical fruit salad

Serves 8–10 Time taken: 15 minutes

If you like tropical fruits, you will like this recipe. It is simple to make and has always proved popular.

- 1 410 g (14½ oz) tin guavas
- 2 397 g (14 oz) tins figs
- 1 565 g (1 lb 4 oz) tin lychees
- 1 425 g (15 oz) tin mangoes
- 1 115 g (4 oz) packet shelled cashew nuts
- 450 ml (¾ pint) fresh orange juice (from tin, carton or jar)
- finely grated rind of 1 lemon
- finely grated rind of 1 orange
- juice of 1–2 lemons
- 3 bananas

Drain the juice from all the tins of fruit and tip the contents into an attractive serving bowl. Leave the mangoes till last as they are soft. Add the cashew nuts and the orange juice followed by the orange and lemon rinds as well as the lemon juice. With a metal spoon give the fruit a careful but thorough mix. Before serving cool it in a refrigerator for a while, and in order to prevent discolouration add the thickish rounds of bananas last and stir the fruit well.

Date and coconut pudding

Serves 4–5

Preparation time: 10 minutes
Baking time: 45 minutes

250 g ($8\frac{3}{4}$ oz) packet of pressed dates (do not use ready cut and sugared dates as they are too sweet)
170 g (6 oz) coarse desiccated coconut
1 egg
300 ml ($\frac{1}{2}$ pint) water
fresh single cream

Unwrap the dates, taking care to remove any cellophane – put under a hot tap for a few moments if you have difficulty. Usually dates from packets are pressed hard together so that a sharp knife is required. Cut the dates into very small cubes. Sometimes the dates have the odd stone so remove that first. It is easier to cut the packet of dates into long strips and then into cubes by cutting them crossways.

Put one third of the dates into a medium-sized soufflé dish. Cover by sprinkling with some coconut and then repeat with dates and coconut twice more so there are three layers of dates with coconut in between.

Now beat the egg lightly in a small bowl and add the water to it gradually, beating all the time.

Preheat oven 190°C, 375°F or Gas No. 5.

Pour the egg and water over the dates. Prick through with a fork in several places to make sure the liquid penetrates the mixture. Put in the oven for 45 minutes. Serve hot with cream.

Note that you can sometimes find ready-cut dates in shops but they are usually sugared and if you use them you will end up with a dessert which is far too sweet.

Nuts and figs dessert

Serves 4–6

Time taken: 12 minutes

This is a perfect combination of figs and nuts but will only appeal to those with a very sweet tooth and those who do not count calories.

1 624 g (1 lb 6 oz) jar nuts in sugar syrup (unripe whole walnuts)
1 397 g (14 oz) golden kadoto figs in syrup
2 tablespoons lemon juice
1 carton single cream

Empty the contents of the jar of nuts into a serving bowl and add the drained juice of figs only at this stage to dilute the thick nut syrup a little. Now take out the nuts, one at a time and with a sharp knife slice them as thinly as you can on a wooden board. Put them back into the dish and add the figs and lemon juice. Give the salad a gentle stir.

Serve chilled with a little fresh cream.

Egg and cream dessert

Serves 4–6 Time taken: 10–15 minutes

This is a useful dessert if one is left with some egg yolks.

4 egg yolks
2 tablespoons castor sugar
1 170 g (6 oz) tin Nestle's cream
1 teaspoon lemon flavouring
5½ teaspoons rum flavouring
grated rind 1 lemon

In an electric mixer or with a hand whisk, beat the egg yolks together with the sugar until light. Add the cream and beat again on a high speed for a few minutes. Reduce speed and pour in the lemon and rum flavourings a little at a time. Cool in a refrigerator for a while and top with lemon rind before serving.

Pancakes with a difference

Serves 4–5 Time taken: 30 minutes

1 packet lemon-flavoured pancake mix which will require the addition of 1 egg
1 500 g (18 oz) packet gooseberry compôte (ready-cooked gooseberries)
2 heaped tablespoons crushed almonds (roasted)
cream (optional)

Read the directions on the packet of pancake mix carefully and make them accordingly.

When the pancakes are ready, open the packet of gooseberry compôte, pour it into a small bowl and stir a little. Now find a suitable flat serving dish in which to build alternate layers of pancakes and gooseberries. Place one pancake in the dish, then spread 1–2 tablespoons of compôte, thoroughly covering the whole surface of the pancake. Carry on piling up all the pancakes and compôte in this way.

Now with a sharp knife, cut the pancake pile, diagonally first then horizontally (between 5–6 times each way), making sure you do not press too hard or else the compôte will come out. Pour the remaining filling all over and sprinkle with the crushed almonds. Serve straight from the dish.

Biscuit crust with lemon filling

Serves 4–6 | Time taken: 20 minutes

115 g (4 oz) butter
½ of 400 g (14¼ oz) packet plain digestive biscuits
3 tablespoons orange juice
packet lemon pie filling which will require the addition of an egg
300 ml (½ pint) water
fresh single cream

First ensure that the butter is soft – don't use it straight from the refrigerator. Crush the biscuits well in a mixing bowl. Rub in the butter with your finger tips until lumps of butter have disappeared and the resulting crumble is even. Add the orange juice, mix well and put the mixture into a shallow tart dish. Press the crumble well into the bottom and sides of the dish. Leave aside.

Follow the instructions on the packet to make the lemon filling. When ready and a little cooler pour it into the crumble biscuit case. Serve when well cooled and set. Add fresh cream.

Strawberry sponge cake

Serves 5–6 | Time taken: 25 minutes

There are several variations to this cake. You can use a chocolate base with a chocolate dessert mix or simply use a different-flavoured mix with the appropriate fruit.

1 185 g (6½ oz) packet sponge cake mixture
1 70 g (2½ oz) packet strawberry-flavoured dessert mix
1 383 g (13½ oz) tin strawberries
1 142 ml (5 fl oz) carton double cream

Open the packet of cake mixture and proceed according to the instructions but remember to set your oven at the right temperature first to save time. Once your mixture is ready tip it into a 20 cm (8 in) sandwich tin and bake the sponge for the required time.

Open the tin of strawberries, prick the cooled sponge (while still in the tin) with a fork and pour a little of the strawberry juice over it – you will not need the rest of the juice for this recipe. Now make the strawberry dessert mix according to the instructions on the packet, pour it in the sandwich tin and over the cake.

When the dessert mix has set, and this usually only takes a few minutes, whisk the cream and decorate the cake using a piping bag and dot with strawberries.

Sponge fingers and lemon dessert

Serves 4–5

Preparation time: 15 minutes
Cooling time: 30 minutes

16 sponge fingers
200 ml (7 fl oz) sweetened grapefruit juice
1 70 g (2½ oz) packet lemon pie filling mix to blend with 1 egg yolk and 300 ml (½ pint) water
juice of ½ lemon
1 egg white
2 dessertspoons sugar
1 142 ml (5 fl oz) carton double cream

You will need an 18 cm (7 in) round cake tin with a loose base.

Lay the sponge fingers side by side on a plate and pour the grapefruit juice evenly over them. Then make the lemon filling according to the instructions on the packet – if there are two sachets in the packet only use one. When the egg yolk and water have been incorporated into the mix and the filling has been brought to the boil and is now thick, stir in the lemon juice. Now whisk the egg white until it is stiff and add the sugar gradually, and at the last minute fold the lemon mixture into the egg white.

The sponge fingers should now have soaked up the grapefruit juice and should be soft – add a little more juice if they are still crunchy. Place half the fingers in the tin, dust with a little sugar followed by half the lemon mixture. Fill the cracks between the fingers with filling. Make another identical layer. Cool in the fridge for 30 minutes then turn out on a dish and cover with whipped cream.

Chestnut sponges with cream

Serves 6

Time taken: 25–30 minutes

8 trifle sponges
150 ml (¼ pint) pure orange juice
1 tablespoon rum flavouring
2 egg whites
1 496 g (1 lb 1½ oz) tin chestnut spread
300 ml (½ pint) double cream
2 dessertspoons sugar
chocolate strands to decorate

Put the trifle sponges on a plate and pour the mixed orange juice and rum flavouring over them. Leave them to one side to soak up the juice. Beat the egg whites until stiff then thoroughly blend in the chestnut purée. Now whip the cream together with the sugar until thick. Line the bottom of a glass dish with a layer of chestnut mixture followed by a layer of cream then some of the sponges. Continue to pile in these ingredients in this order until you've used them all up.

Fill all the cracks between the sponges with generous amounts of chestnut and cream and finish off with a layer of cream. Sprinkle chocolate strands over the top to decorate. Cool on the top shelf of the fridge for 15–20 minutes.

Sponge fingers and peaches

Serves 4–6

Time taken: 15–20 minutes

1 822 g (1 lb 13 oz) peach slices in syrup
1 packet of 16 sponge fingers

For the sauce:
½ dessertspoon custard powder
½ teaspoon ground cinnamon
6–8 tablespoons white or rosé wine
½ teaspoon lemon essence
fresh cream

Open the tin of peaches and drain off the juice and put aside. In a shallow dish, spread out 8 sponge fingers evenly and fill the gaps between them with peaches. Repeat this arrangement for the second layer and place the remaining peaches round the dish.

Now make the sauce: put the custard powder, the cinnamon as well as a little bit of the peach juice in a saucepan and stir well until the mixture is completely smooth. Then add the rest of the juice to avoid lumps. When the colour starts to change and the mixture begins to bubble add the wine very gradually and the lemon essence. Go on stirring for a minute or so and then remove from the heat. Pour the liquid over the fingers and peaches and allow to cool before putting in a refrigerator to set. Serve with fresh cream.

Sponge flan with cherries and cream

Serves 4–5

Time taken: 10 minutes

Flan cases (they come in several sizes) are very useful if there is little time to make an elaborate dessert. They can be served on all occasions – at childrens' parties (without the Drambuie!) or at other gatherings. If you are entertaining large numbers, different fruit fillings such as peaches, gooseberries, strawberries, etc. can be used.

1 14 cm (5½ in) flan case
3 tablespoons Drambuie or other liqueur
1 425 g (15 oz) tin black cherries in heavy syrup
142 ml (5 fl oz) carton double cream
1 tablespoon crushed nuts

Prick the flan in the middle as well as the side with a fork and pour the Drambuie slowly and evenly all over. Open the cherry tin and spoon a little of the juice over the side of the flan as this part is particularly thick and should be moist. Place the cherries and the rest of the juice in the case and cover with lightly whipped cream. Sprinkle the crushed nuts all over.

Pineapple sponge dessert

Serves 12 and over   Time taken: 30 minutes

This is a rich and creamy dessert which will serve quite a few people and which will taste even better if made in advance.

2 18 cm (7 in) flan cases
170 g (6 oz) unsalted butter
255 g (9 oz) sugar
1 capful vanilla flavouring essence
3 capfuls lemon flavouring essence
100 ml (3½ fl oz) pineapple juice from a tin
4 eggs
2 142 ml (5 fl oz) cartons double cream
crushed almonds to decorate

Split the 2 flan cases into 4 layers and find a deep glass dish in which they'll fit.

In a mixer thoroughly cream the butter and 200 g of the sugar then add the vanilla and lemon flavourings and the pineapple juice. Separate the eggs and blend the yolks one by one into the butter cream and beat well. Now beat the egg whites until stiff and incorporate the rest of the sugar a little at a time. Whip the cream until thick and fold into the egg whites followed by the butter cream. Mix all the ingredients (by hand) well together. Line the bottom of the bowl with some of the mixture then place a sponge half over it. Spread some more mixture on top of the sponge and alternate sponge and cream until you've used everything up. You can afford to be generous with the mixture – so fill all the gaps as you build up this dessert. Sprinkle with the crushed almonds. Put on the coldest shelf of the fridge to cool or if you have a freezer and you're in a hurry, put it in there instead for a little while. Serve straight from the glass dish.

Victoria sponge cake with fillings

There are numerous brands of sponge cake mixes on the market and they are useful standbys should unexpected guests turn up. You will find here a few assorted recipes for fillings which could be used in a Victoria sandwich. We have used 2 18 cm (7 in) cake tins for all four recipes but as the fillings are on the generous side 2 22 cm (8½ in) tins could be used instead providing you worked with two packets of sponge mix.

For the sponge in all cases you will need: 1 184 g (6½ oz) packet sponge mix and the addition of an egg. Milk and sugar could be required as well.

Start preparing the mix following the directions on the packet. Once the mixture is ready divide it equally between the two tins then put them into the hot oven. When the sponges are ready and have cooled down a little fill with any of the four fillings.

Pineapple filling

Serves 4–5 Time taken: 20–30 minutes

1 250 g (8¾ oz) tin crushed pineapple
1 tablespoon butter
1½ tablespoons lemon juice
2 dessertspoons cornflour
150 ml (¼ pint) water
1 egg yolk
2 dessertspoons sugar

Put the crushed pineapple, the butter and the lemon juice in a pan. Blend the cornflour with a little of the water and add it to the pan together with the rest of the water. In a separate small bowl beat the egg yolk then stir it into the mixture. Cook on a low heat until thick then add the sugar. This filling is quite lemony and you may like a little more sugar.

Loganberry filling

Serves 4–5 Time taken: 20–30 minutes

1 410 g (14½ oz) tin loganberries
150 ml (¼ pint) double cream
2 dessertspoons sugar

Drain the loganberries but keep the juice as you may like to use it later to make a hot sauce. Mash the loganberries with a fork – this will be easy as they are soft.

In a separate bowl whip the cream until very thick (but make sure it doesn't turn to butter) together with the sugar. Now fold the loganberries into the cream and spoon out the mixture on to the sponge. If you wish to serve a hot sauce with this cake, dissolve a little cornflour in some of the loganberry juice. Then put it together with the rest of the juice in a saucepan and cook on a low heat until it thickens.

Coffee filling

Serves 4–5 | Time taken: 20–30 minutes

This filling is perfect if you are entertaining friends to coffee and cakes – it is quite sweet and goes very well with a cup of coffee.

50 g (2 oz) butter
115 g (4 oz) icing sugar
1 egg yolk
1 tablespoon top of milk
1 dessertspoon Camp coffee and chicory essence

For the icing, if required:
170 g (6 oz) icing sugar
1 egg white
1 dessertspoon Camp coffee and chicory essence
walnuts to decorate

In an electric mixer or by hand, cream together the soft butter and icing sugar. Beat in the egg yolk followed by the milk and the coffee essence. Sandwich the mixture between the sponges and then make the icing. Put the icing sugar in a mixing bowl then make a well in the centre and drop the egg in. Whip for a few minutes, then add the coffee essence a little at a time. Spread the icing over the cake and round it, smoothing it down with a cake slice or knife. Leave it to set for a while. Decorate with walnuts. As an alternative and if you don't like icing, you could cover the cake with whipped cream.

Orange butter cream filling

Serves 4–5 | Time taken: 20–30 minutes

2 egg yolks
5 tablespoons double cream
a pinch of flour
63 g (2½ oz) butter
63 g (2½ oz) vanilla sugar
150 ml (¼ pint) fresh orange juice

Put the orange juice in a saucepan and cook on a low heat until it has reduced to 2 tablespoons.

Place the yolks, the cream and the flour in a bowl and put the bowl in a saucepan of hot water and cook the mixture on a low heat until thick. Set aside to cool. Cream the butter in a mixer or by hand then blend the vanilla sugar in. Now add the egg and cream mixture a little at a time to the butter cream, whilst beating all the while. Add the cold reduced orange juice to the mixture to finish the butter cream.

Index